DOWN HOME COOKIN'
WITHOUT THE DOWN HOME FAT

by
Dawn Hall

Chosen as one of the "Best of the Best" in Ohio by
Gwen McKee & Barbara Moseley of Quail Ridge Press/QRP Books
"Best of the Best" Cookbook Series

The <u>extremely</u> low-fat, fast and easy recipe
book for <u>busy</u> people.

Cozy Homestead Publishing
Cozy Homestead Publishing, Inc.
Swanton, Ohio

DOWN HOME COOKIN'
WITHOUT THE DOWN HOME FAT

by
Dawn Hall

Edited by Cynthia Beekley
Recipes computer-analyzed by Diane Yantiss
Photos by Dennis Clark—October 1995
Book and Cover Design by Dawn Hall and
    Diane Mennitt-White
Typesetting by Beaver Pond Publishing and Printing,
    Greenville, PA
Library of Congress Number: 95-83465
ISBN#: 0-9649950-0-X

Attention Businesses, Groups and Teachers; This book is
available at quantity discounts with bulk purchase for
business, educational or sales promotional use. For more
information call, write or fax:

Cozy Homestead Publishing

Cozy Homestead Publishing, Inc.
5425 S. Fulton-Lucas Road
Swanton, Ohio 43558
Phone: 419-826-COOK (2665)
FAX: 419-826-2700

♥♥♥♥♥♥♥♥♥♥♥♥♥♥♥♥♥♥♥♥♥♥♥♥♥♥

Table of Contents

This *"Kids Cookin'"* logo next to a recipe means the recipe is *"child appropriate"*. Most children will be able to make this recipe with a minimum of adult supervision.

♥♥♥♥♥♥♥♥♥♥♥♥♥♥♥♥♥♥♥♥♥♥♥♥♥♥

♥♥♥♥♥♥♥♥♥♥♥♥♥♥♥♥♥♥♥♥♥♥♥♥♥♥♥♥♥

"We truly can enjoy good food that is also low in fat. The recipes in Down HOME Cookin' are perfect examples of just such recipes."

—Jo Anna Lund
Food Writer and Author
Healthy Exchanges, Inc.

"This cookbook has been a wonderful tool for people trying to adjust to their new lifestyle after their cardiac event."

—Samantha Christie, RN
Cardiac Rehab Nurse

"As a leader for First Peace (a diet class), Dawn Hall's cookbook has been a valuable tool in helping my ladies lose weight and very successfully, also! Our potluck rule is just bring anything out of 'Down Home Cookin without the Fat!'"

—Kathy Rahla
Leader, First Peace
(weight loss class)

"The Down Home Cookin' Cookbook has been a Godsend. My family has truly enjoyed the unique recipes. They are easy to prepare and healthy for you. They have helped reduce the fat in our diets which in turn is helping us to lose weight.

—Cheryl A Oedy
Homemaker

NutraSweet®

NutraSweet® Hotline
1-800-321-7254
from 8 a.m. to 5 p.m. Central Time

♥♥♥♥♥♥♥♥♥♥♥♥♥♥♥♥♥♥♥♥♥♥♥♥♥♥♥♥♥

♥♥♥♥♥♥♥♥♥♥♥♥♥♥♥♥♥♥♥♥♥♥♥♥♥♥♥♥♥

Thank you! Thank you!! Thank you!!!

I full heartedly believe this book is a gift from God, so of course I want to thank Him first of all.

Second, I want to thank my sweet, kind, and wonderful husband, Tracy, who never complained about all of the flops I created. I know I owe him at least $1,000 for all of the food I've ruined. Trust me! Putting together fat-free ingredients does not always guarantee a flavorful recipe! Anyone who knows me knows how frugal I am. If he had complained, I would've probably quit, but he never did. I love him all the more for being so supportive. Thank you, Sweetheart!

A big thank you to all of my students in my water aerobics and W.O.W. (Watching Our Weight) classes who constantly encouraged me to start writing this cookbook. It was their consistent request for more of my recipes and overwhelming approval of them that made me more appreciative of my God-given creative cooking talents. (In the past I'd taken that for granted.)

To all of my friends, family and students, thank you for being my taste-tester guinea pigs! I appreciate your truthfulness in letting me know which ones you liked and did not like. It's a very rewarding feeling knowing every single recipe in this book tastes delicious and has received your "tasty seal of approval".

On behalf of my family and me, I cannot express how overwhelmingly thankful we are to everyone who was a part of our "angel network" and intervened on our behalf to sell the first 18,000 copies of my recipe book within 2½ months...all by word of mouth! With all of our hearts, "Thank you so very much!" It is because of all of you and the request from the public for more that we now offer this second edition.

There are two Godly woman authors of terrific cookbooks I want to publicly thank. I want to publicly, because in a self-centered world of "me, me, me" these two women exemplify truly Godly, professional business women who are confident enough in their own capabilities to offer a helping hand to "a new girl on the block" in the industry. It is with the utmost respect and admiration that I thank JoAnna Lund of "Healthy Exchanges" for her wisdom, guidance and direction. It is only after serious thought and prayer of her insightful counsel that I followed through with this book. Thank You, JoAnna!

Also a warm thank you to Pam Mycoskie, author of "Butter Busters Cookbook" and "I'm listening". It was her idea of using a red gingham cover and having our family photo done in denim with bandanas. I love both ideas! I can't thank Pam without

♥♥♥♥♥♥♥♥♥♥♥♥♥♥♥♥♥♥♥♥♥♥♥♥♥♥♥♥♥

♥♥♥♥♥♥♥♥♥♥♥♥♥♥♥♥♥♥♥♥♥♥♥♥♥♥♥♥

thanking her wonderful husband Mike also. Being with them is like being with ol' (not old!) friends, even though we've only had dinner together once. They barely know me, yet I really believe they have my best interest in mind. I thank them for their knowledge, insight and most of all their sincere, caring love towards my family and me.

A special thank you to Cynthia Beekley, my Editor. (She was also my favorite English teacher.)

To my dear, photogenic friends Bill Harris and Andrea Yabarra who were perfect models for my front cover, thanks so much! You were my first choices and I'm thrilled that you could do it!

I can not thank Container Graphics Corporation enough for the fabulous job they've done putting my book's cover together. Container Graphics' leadership and staffed positions are people with high integrity and superior talent. To know them is to love them. It has been my honor and privilege to work hands-on with them every step of the way. I am forever grateful. An extra special heartfelt thank you to the following people for going the extra mile for me: Bill Beaker, Dave Crawford, Dan Bidel, Diane Mennitt-White and last but not least Dennis Clark, the photographer.

I also want to say thank you to Rich Faler of Beaver Pond Publishing for being a mentor to me in the publishing field. His patience is appreciated.

As you can see the Lord has had His hands involved with this book from the very beginning. It's to Him I give all the praise and glory for the success of this book. I am just so thankful that He has chosen me to work through to bring it to you! I am also extremely thankful to everyone He has worked through to help me with it!

Thanks again everybody!

♥ *Abbreviations* ♥

c.	=	cup
Tbs.	=	Tablespoon
tsp.	=	teaspoon
pkg.	=	package
pkgs.	=	packages
oz.	=	ounces
lb.	=	pound
lbs.	=	pounds

♥♥♥♥♥♥♥♥♥♥♥♥♥♥♥♥♥♥♥♥♥♥♥♥♥♥♥♥

♥♥♥♥♥♥♥♥♥♥♥♥♥♥♥♥♥♥♥♥♥♥♥♥♥♥♥♥

About the Author

I feel like I was born on a diet! I can't remember a time when I didn't have to watch my weight. At times it felt like all I had to do was look at a page of a magazine ad with fattening delicious looking food on it and I'd gain 5 lbs. Needless to say, for me, watching my weight has been very, very frustrating. I wish I could tell you, now that I've written this book, that my weight is no longer a challenge for me, but it still is. However, maintaining a comfortable weight for myself is much, much easier than before, now that I've learned to cook the healthier way. But I will still never be skinny. Healthy and fit, yes...skinny, no!

Things really turned around for me when I realized that the dictionary definition for the word "diet" was not starvation or depravation! Diet is what we consume by food or liquid. Everyone eats a diet. The key is, what does yours and mine consist of?

From then on, I have never been on a "diet." Yes, I watch what I eat and when I want to lose a few extra fat pounds I increase my walking or aerobic time and cut back on the amount of calories. But I keep eating the same foods all the time. I know that what I need to lose excess fat is what I need to keep eating to maintain my weight. I know I'll never be a "skinny-minny". But at the same time I feel relieved to know I don't have to fear being a "fatty-patty" anymore either!

It says in the Bible to "Train your children in the ways they should go." I believe that it's not only about spiritual things, but also about all things, including physical. The saying "we are what we eat" has a lot of validity to it. And wouldn't it be nice if it were as easy as "if you don't want to be fat, don't eat fat". There are loads and loads of fat-free and low-fat products flooding the market today, but nonetheless they're as fattening as can be, loaded down with all those sugars and sweeteners! It's true you can eat more "quantity" of food (gram vs. gram) when you eat fat-free, low-fat foods vs. high fat foods. But the truth is if you're eating 3,000 calories of fat-free food or 3,000 calories of high fat foods the total of calories is the same and you can get fat!

♥♥♥♥♥♥♥♥♥♥♥♥♥♥♥♥♥♥♥♥♥♥♥♥♥♥♥♥

Calories are calories! The ultimate sad truth is we need to lower the amount of total calories our bodies keep daily. We can do that by increasing our aerobic lengths of time, decreasing our intake of calories, or both. Yes, it is easier to lower your chances of eating more calories by eating fat-free and low-fat foods. But nonetheless, if you're eating too many calories, you're eating too many calories and you won't lose fat. Too much of any good thing—even fat-free, low-fat food is...you guessed it: too much!!!

Don't get me wrong, I don't encourage eating high-fat foods by any means whatsoever! I'm strongly against it! But I just want to set the record straight that eating too much, no matter how healthy it is for you is eating too much, period. It's a hard fact to swallow, but it is the truth. Moderation is the key. That's something I still work on, on a daily basis. Remembering that moderation is the key enables me to enjoy foods (I used to never allow myself to eat) without feeling total guilt and shame. You know what I'm talking about! Occasionally, I give myself freedom to wander in moderation! An occasional piece of chocolate or a few potato chips, making a conscious choice that "I'm choosing to wander." Another important factor is that consciously choosing to wander from a low-fat, high fiber, healthy diet is something that is

occasionally done in "moderation." Special occasions, holidays, etc. are prime examples of times when we may "choose to wander". But choosing to wander doesn't mean going "hog-wild" and eating all the chips, hot dogs, regular sodas and sweets we would like until our hearts content. It means choosing to have a little of something that would normally not be eaten on a daily basis. Realize which foods are "trouble" foods for you. Trouble foods are foods that I say "get me goin" —foods that are hard to stop eating once you get going on them. And what may be a "trouble" food for you, may not be a trouble food for someone else. Don't buy "trouble foods," even if they're for someone else in the family. Why? Even if you're feeling strong when you buy them and you have every intention of not eating them, when your guard is down and you're feeling weak that "trouble food", is going to be pounding, begging and screaming at you to indulge in "just a little piece". Before you know it you may have consumed numerous little pieces. And what do you know? Whammy! Guilt city! It's just not worth it! Know and learn your weaknesses. Knowing our weaknesses helps us to grow into stronger and better human beings.

I love to create! The first year we were married, my husband and I never ate the same thing for dinner twice. I took pride in never allowing my husband's meals to be boring. On our first wedding anniversary we asked each other what we could do to become a better spouse. My husband, Tracy, said "Honey could you just cook the same meal twice, at least once this year?" We laughed! Here my meat and potatoes man wanted plain ol' meals!

About Heart & Hand

Few things have given me greater joy in life than knowing our family is trying to make a positive difference in the inner city of Toledo by being involved with the Heart & Hand program. With a hands-on involvement Pastor Keith and his wonderful wife Shannon focus on the needs of the central city, crossing over both racial and economic barriers.

Through their kids church program for children and their youth group for teens they are establishing a moral foundation for the future generation based on Biblical principles.

We are in constant need of bus drivers to transport children to the programs, as well as more volunteers to help in many other areas. Last but not least, child sponsors are needed.

Heart & Hand is supported financially through tax-deductible gifts and child sponsorship. What is a child sponsor? A child sponsor is someone who supports Heart & Hand with $24.00 per month and has the opportunity to have personal contact with his sponsored child in order to be a positive influence in his or her life.

For information contact:

Keith Stepp
Heart & Hand
1630 Broadway
Toledo, Ohio 43609

or call:
419-244-7020

A portion of the book's proceeds is going towards Toledo's Heart & Hand Outreach Program. On behalf of all of the children, thank you very much for your support!

Sincerely,
Dawn

❤❤❤❤❤❤❤❤❤❤❤❤❤❤❤❤❤❤❤❤❤❤❤❤❤

Well! What about Fat?

Fat! Fat! Fat! Aren't you sick of it? It can be frustrating to live with it, and you can't live without it! I'm not a doctor, nor do I intend to sound like one. I do have a lot of personal experience with the yucky stuff though. As a recovering compulsive eater myself and as an aerobic instructor and a facilitator of self-help groups such as W.O.W. (Watching Our Weight), I do know quite a bit about fat. As a teacher it seems only natural that I desire to share with you briefly in layman's terms what I know about fat. So I'm going to K.I.S.S. the subject lightly. (K.I.S.S. = Keep It Simple, Sweetie!)

Our bodies do need fat (approx. 10 grams per day) for healthy skin, hair, nails, etc. Ten grams is such a tiny bit that most of us can consume the fats we need naturally without *ever* adding a bit of fat to the preparation of our food—*ever!* I don't even have oil, real butter, margarine, Crisco, etc. in our home. We just don't need it! Yes, there are good fats and bad fats, regarding cholesterol, but the truth is fats are fattening no matter what type of fat. Although olive oil is less harmful than margarine, butter, Crisco and other fats, it is still not good for you. Dietary fat (foods that we eat that have fat in them) is the most concentrated form of calories. Fats have 9 calories per gram versus protein or carbohydrates that have 4 calories per gram, and alcohol which has 7 calories per gram. A gram is a weight measurement. Refraining from fats, ounce for ounce, you can consume a larger quantity of food for your calories. Dietary fat is also more easily turned into body fat once eaten because, of all the calories, it is most like our bodies' fat. Now you know how the saying "over the lips onto the hips" came into effect! For the heart-conscious, health-conscious and weight-conscious person, avoiding dietary fat is helpful (but not the cure-all) for maintaining a healthy desirable weight. More of that coming up.

Most people know that lowering their fat intake is helpful in reducing heart disease. Heart disease has had a drastic reduction since the public has been made more aware of this fact. Once again the statement "we are what we eat" has a lot of validity. Choosing to "wander" occasionally is okay just as long as it does not become the "norm." Science has proven you can even reverse heart disease with a 10% fat diet.

What a lot of people are not aware of is cancer thrives on fats, too! Cancer is the generic name given to over 100 different diseases, which have a common factor: they like fats and refined sugars. Reducing your consumption of fats lowers not only your risk of heart disease, but also cancer.

❤❤❤❤❤❤❤❤❤❤❤❤❤❤❤❤❤❤❤❤❤❤❤❤❤

❤❤❤❤❤❤❤❤❤❤❤❤❤❤❤❤❤❤❤❤❤❤❤❤❤

Aunt Dawn's Tricks of the Trade

No matter what line of work you are in, you know that there are "tricks" that make your job a little easier. Here are a few of mine.....

F irst thing you've got to do is "DEFAT" the house! I know this is tough! I did it too when I first started eating extremely low fat. But listen to me. These are wise words, "You gotta do it!" There's no if's, and's or but's about it! Fat is not good for you, it's not good for your children and I don't care if your spouse is as skinny as a rail! He doesn't need it either! Fat is fat. Period! Get it out. Mayo, Crisco, oils, high junk food, high fatty red meats! Pitch it! Believe me as a penny counter all my life I know it's hard throwing away that money. All I can say is "Just Do It!" It's going to cost you a lot more in the long run (mentally, emotionally and physically) if you don't.

Second—Go to your favorite grocery store and stock up on fat-free products. There are many to choose from. Enclosed in this book are my favorites. Easy rule of thumb, if there are more than 3 grams of fat per 100 calories, don't eat it. To be honest with you I think that's even Too Much but the American Heart Association says 30% or less intake of dietary fat. Personally I try to stick to 20 grams of fat a day. Which is approximately about 10% of my calories per day. For optimum health that is what I encourage for myself.

If you can't "COLD DUCK IT" then make your changes gradually. Milk is a biggy. A lot of people who've grown up on whole milk have a hard time making the switch to skim. Here is what I encourage my classes to do if they're having a hard time making the switch.

1st week   ¹/₂ whole milk and ¹/₂ - 2% milk mixed
2nd week 2% milk
3rd week   ¹/₂ - 2% milk and ¹/₂ - 1% milk
4th week   1% milk
5th week   ¹/₂ - 1% milk and ¹/₂ skim milk
6th week   skim milk!

There that wasn't so bad after all—was it?

Surprising Fact
Whole Milk — Approximately ¹/₂ fat!
2% Milk   — Approximately ¹/₃ fat
Skim Milk — 0 fat!!!!   WOW!!!

❤❤❤❤❤❤❤❤❤❤❤❤❤❤❤❤❤❤❤❤❤❤❤❤

♥♥♥♥♥♥♥♥♥♥♥♥♥♥♥♥♥♥♥♥♥♥♥♥♥♥♥

- When cooking, chew mint gum. It helps keep me from tasting. (If that doesn't work, tape your mouth shut!)

- Hurry! Wash off those fingers! <u>Don't lick them clean!</u>

- If you're journaling daily what you eat, add 25 calories per small taste of low fat food and 50 calories per taste for high fat foods! You'll be surprised how fast those calories add up!

- Plan on spending 1 hour each week cleaning fresh veggies and fruits after grocery shopping. I can guarantee having veggies and fruit prepared for easy eating will increase consumption dramatically! Let's face it, usually when you want a quick snack the last thing you feel like doing is peeling a carrot! A clever idea I do is cut up into bite size pieces my veggies for salads and put them in a relish tray. I refrigerate prepared veggies so when I'm preparing a salad all I have to do is sprinkle whatever veggies I want onto the salad.

- Take a large plastic cake container (Rubbermaid or Tupperware, etc.) and turn it upside down. Using 3 large heads of dark green lettuces, (leafy, romaine, etc.) prepare a large salad of <u>greens</u> only. Only garnish with bite-sized veggies prepared in relish tray (mentioned earlier) once ready to serve salad.

- For relishes I cut the veggies into "finger food" size, and put into another relish tray. For quick dips I use favorite salad dressings.

- Fruits—fresh melons, pineapples and berries can be cleaned and stored for up to 5-6 days. I also like to put these in relish trays; Zip-Loc bags work fine also. Only allow fresh fruits to sit out on the counter. Hopefully a healthy fresh visual will be more enticing than an ol' prepackaged processed snack. (If not, at least it was a good try!)

- I encourage people who are trying to live a healthier life style to express their needs in what I call a "win-win" way, assertively. Assertively expressing your needs allows people to know what your needs are while respecting where they are in life. (In a paragraph ahead I share my Kruncher's Bar-B-Que Chips story.) Assertive communication means being open and honest in a thoughtful and tactful way. The "Golden Rule" (treat others the way you want to be treated) is a great rule of thumb when expressing your needs.

- Studies show that people who are most successful at maintaining a healthier life style are those who have a strong

♥♥♥♥♥♥♥♥♥♥♥♥♥♥♥♥♥♥♥♥♥♥♥♥♥♥♥

♥♥♥♥♥♥♥♥♥♥♥♥♥♥♥♥♥♥♥♥♥♥♥♥♥♥

support system. If your friends and family won't be there for you, then consider belonging to a self-help group who will.

• If someone absolutely insists on having something that is totally fattening and practically irresistible for you in the house, then by all means be honest with them and assertively ask them to hide it and not eat it in front of you. My husband used to love Krunchers Bar-B-Que chips. The problem was I did too! I eat 12 chips and gain 10 pounds (okay—maybe I really don't, but it feels like it!) And anyway—who can eat only 12? I asked him to keep them in his truck. That way he has them for his lunch and I'm not being tortured by some measly little 5 ounce bag screaming from my pantry "Eat Me! Eat Me!"

• Moderation is the key. To say I'll never eat a Bar-B-Que Kruncher chip in my life is to set myself up for failure. Remember you can choose to wander. Just don't make wandering a habit.

• Another trick that gets me through challenging times (when I'm away from home) is keeping fat-free snacks in the trunk of my car. Because I do this I don't have to worry about being at a carry-out's or gas station's mercy. By keeping a variety of fat-free snacks I like in the trunk, I always know that I'm prepared if I become hungry. However, I do NOT "eat and drive". If I do eat something from the trunk, I make myself take a few moments, turn the car off and sit in the car. I make myself "enjoy the moment". Let's face it. Eating is orally stimulating. While eating your body releases chemicals that bring about a calming effect. (It's easy to see why people become food addicts.) When we eat we are not only feeding a hungry body, there are other factors also. When we "eat on the run" we deprive ourself of the complete eating experience. To avoid overeating, do not eat while driving or while watching T.V.

• Prepare only as much as you think you will eat. Serve appropriate portions by putting food on plates. Serving family style (with bowls on the table) encourages overeating. Let's face it. Haven't we all at one time or another eaten a second helping of something just because it was there staring us in the face and it tasted good?

• Make a double of what you'll need and freeze the remaining portion for a "quick meal" down the road.

• When I worked full time, I liked cooking for the week on Saturdays. It saved me time and with microwaves was convenient.

♥♥♥♥♥♥♥♥♥♥♥♥♥♥♥♥♥♥♥♥♥♥♥♥♥♥

♥♥♥♥♥♥♥♥♥♥♥♥♥♥♥♥♥♥♥♥♥♥♥♥♥♥

I'M SICK OF THE LIES!!!

Manufacturers know that people want to eat healthier nowadays and are more health conscious. So what do the manufacturers do to us? A lot of them lie! (Lie! Lie! Lie!) And I'm sick of it!!! I've had enough!!!

I'm going to tell you in layman's terms the ins and outs of reading a nutrition label on the side of the box. Don't take the manufacturer's word that the product is "low-fat" unless you READ the nutrition label first! This is an absolute must! For those of you who are hard of learning, repeat after me:

> "I, _____(put your name here)_____will not buy any product without first looking at the nutrition label on the package! As a responsible person I am going to know up-front exactly how many fats and calories I will be consuming. I am not going to fall for their lies!!!"

> _____.
>
> (signature here)

Good! Now we're on our way to success!

First of all, let's know up front that I'm talking primarily about fats. I'm not talking about sodium: I encourage trying not to add table salt onto prepared foods because we get more than enough naturally in the foods we eat. And I am not addressing fiber, of which we should try to get at least 25-30 grams per day. My primary focus here is fats.

Believe me (I don't lie) when I tell you "things are not always as they are perceived to be."

Perfect example: Kraft Macaroni and Cheese. The kind you add milk to. Terrible—right? Wrong! As far as fats it's okay as boxed. A 5.5 ounce box has 2 servings in it—which is a nice sized portion, 260 calories per serving and only 3 grams of fat total. What makes it fattening is when we add the milk and margarine. If we would use fat free margarine or liquid Butter Buds and skim milk the fat calories would remain low.

On the other hand, so-called healthy products such as convenient microwave meals that claim to be low fat can be high in fat with up to 9 grams of fat for one small meal! Check it out!

Another thing that cracks me up is the portion size. Even some authors of so-called low fat cookbooks get their fats and calories low per serving because they reduce the normal portion size serving down to some inky-dinky piece! PLEASE!!! We're not birds! If you're eating a so-called low-fat dessert and it was

♥♥♥♥♥♥♥♥♥♥♥♥♥♥♥♥♥♥♥♥♥♥♥♥♥♥

♥♥♥♥♥♥♥♥♥♥♥♥♥♥♥♥♥♥♥♥♥♥♥♥♥♥♥♥

made in a 9" x 13" pan, and the recipe says it has 36 servings you can bet your bottom dollar that's an itty bitty serving size! (I would call it a taste—not a serving!) Yes, it may be slightly under 100 calories, but multiply that by the number of servings you'll probably eat to be satisfied (2-3) and you've just eaten almost 200-300 calories! Again, don't be fooled! Check out your portion size!

"Aunt Dawn's Antidotes" for Overall Health

• Wake up at least five minutes earlier than you need to. Thank God for things and spend time with our Higher Power. Praise Him—even if you don't want to. Praising God will lift your spirits. It helps you start your day with the right attitude.

• Take a few moments and *visualize* yourself succeeding in taking overall good care of yourself. Visualize yourself eating low-fat snacks and meals, and feeling satisfied. Also visualize yourself exercising regularly. Remember: what you think about, you bring about!

• Take time for at least ½ hour of *exercise* (aerobically) at least 3 times a week, if not more. This is a perfect time for building relationships also! I think a lot less people would need to go to counselors and therapists if we'd just take time to share our feelings with a good friend. To have a friend you have to be a friend. I find walking and talking to a good friend extremely wonderful. It's like getting a two for one deal! Also, personally— I like to cross train: (Do a different exercise daily.) walk, bike, dance or step aerobics. It gives spice to my life. Studies show people who like the exercise they're doing are more apt to stick with it! The key is find what you enjoy doing and do it.

• Time Management. Don't overbook. If you think it's going to take 10 minutes to get there, give yourself 15 so you aren't under so much pressure. (I have to work on this one daily. As an overachiever I tend to overbook—which is extremely stressful!) Teach yourself to relax and seize the moment!

• Think only positive thoughts. If it's not positive <u>get rid of that thought</u> right away! Negative thoughts can bring you down without you even realizing it! Don't <u>EVEN</u> give room to them! Life is too short to be wasting time being negative. And don't EVEN hang around negative people who bring you down. Life is a positive gift that negativity (if allowed) will rip apart and tear to shreds! Don't allow anything or anybody to deprive you of your happiness because of their negativity.

♥♥♥♥♥♥♥♥♥♥♥♥♥♥♥♥♥♥♥♥♥♥♥♥♥♥

♥♥♥♥♥♥♥♥♥♥♥♥♥♥♥♥♥♥♥♥♥♥♥♥♥

Grocery Shopping

The supermarket can be a dreadful experience if you don't prepare yourself. Besides watching labels and following a grocery list, here are some "tricks of the trade" regarding grocery shopping.

• Carry a basket instead of pushing a cart if you don't need a lot of items. With your arms full of products you are less likely to buy compulsively.

• If you are pushing a cart, leave it at the end of the aisle if you only need one or two items in an aisle that normally would be considered a "danger zone". (You know what I mean. The aisles that are loaded with high-fat, scrumptious, tantalizing products that are hard to resist.) At times it even seems like those hard-to-resist products are calling out to you by name, saying, "Buy me! Buy me! You know you want me!" I hate those aisles! Wouldn't it be nice and a whole lot less stressful if all supermarket aisles were as easy to go down as the cleaning supply or paper products aisle? If you don't push your cart down that horrendous fat-loaded aisle, then you will be a lot less likely to grab other products since your hands will be full carrying what you need. The goal is when you come to an aisle like that, get in and out of there as soon as possible! Put blinders on and go directly to the product you're looking for! Don't dillydally.

• If you see your favorite "weakness" high fat item on sale walk as fast as you can away from it!
Let's pretend we see our favorite chocolate bar on sale. It's an unbelievable sale! 1,000 candy bars (remember these are your favorite) for only a buck! Oh my gosh! You can't believe it! It's only natural to start to rationalize giving in to this absolutely fabulous temptation... "I'll only eat $1/4$ of a bar (which is only about 3 grams of fat) for the next 11 years. Yeah! That's a good idea!" Come on now! Be honest! I'm sure I'm not the only one in the world who debates with herself regarding high fat items I know I shouldn't buy! I call a situation like this a "Red flag". Whenever you see a potential red-flag, beware! Tell yourself, "no!" And again—get away from it as soon as possible.
Hopefully the old saying "Out of sight, out of mind" will be true. If you give into that moment of weakness, believe me: you'll regret it! You're paying way too high a price ($1.00 for this situation) for a lot of grief, frustration, anxiety and stress! Do yourself a favor! Don't buy it!

• Watch prices! Manufacturers love to market products as fat-free and then double the price! Often you can find a similar

♥♥♥♥♥♥♥♥♥♥♥♥♥♥♥♥♥♥♥♥♥♥♥♥♥

♥♥♥♥♥♥♥♥♥♥♥♥♥♥♥♥♥♥♥♥♥♥♥♥♥♥

product for a lot less! I refuse to pay double just because it has 1 gram of fat less than a less expensive product. Pretzel manufacturers love to do this. Compare and save.

Saving Money With Coupons

Let's face it, for the most part fat-free products are more expensive than their counterparts. I feel it's worth peace of mind, and better health, to pay the extra. When I have time, I do "the coupon thing". For a $5.00 investment, my coupon book has saved me a lot of grief, time and money. I get so many compliments on my coupon organization and it is <u>so much</u> less stressful than sorting through them that I'm sharing it with you. Here's what you'll need:

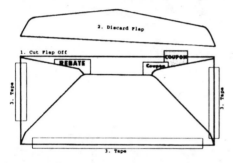

- 100 page large photo album with clear film sheets (that hold photos in place)
- 1 envelope with flap cut off
- tape
- coupons
- tabs (used for filing)

Label tabs individually for easy finding. I label mine: Dairy, Breads, Meats, Fish, Chicken, Cleaning supplies, Hair care, etc. Each section will have its own title page. Tape labelled tabs onto outside edge of photo album pages so that you can easily go to any section desired. (Only one tab per page. There will be numerous pages without tabs in each section following title page.)

Put cut out coupons in proper sections.

Cut flap off of envelope. Tape envelope to front inside cover of photo album. Put coupons you've pulled from designated section in envelope for easy storage until check out time. I also put rebates into the envelope.

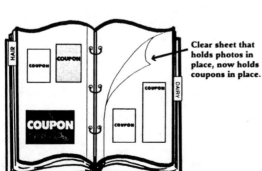

Clear sheet that holds photos in place, now holds coupons in place.

♥♥♥♥♥♥♥♥♥♥♥♥♥♥♥♥♥♥♥♥♥♥♥♥♥

♥♥♥♥♥♥♥♥♥♥♥♥♥♥♥♥♥♥♥♥♥♥♥♥♥♥

What I like to stock in my kitchen

There are literally hundreds (if not thousands) of fat-free and very-low fat products on the market now. The problem (as I'm sure a lot of you know) is that many do NOT taste good! The other day I tried a new fat-free potato chip. Yuck! I'm telling you, the bag it was packaged in had to taste better than the product! It was terrible!

Have no fear, Aunt Dawn is here! The following is a list of products I enjoy using. Look for them in your grocery store with confidence that they'll taste better than the packaging!

An easy rule of thumb when looking on labels is: if it has more than 3 grams of fat per 100 calories don't buy it, don't use it and pitch it! The only time I break that rule is for super lean beef such as:

Type of Beef	Serving Size	Fat grams	Calories	%fat calories
London Broil/Flank Steak	3 oz.	6	167	32%
Top Loin-Lean Only	3 oz.	6	162	33%
Eye of Round (As a steak, roast or have butcher grind for super lean hamburger)	3 oz.	5	150	30

Healthy Choice used to have a very low (4 gr. of fat per 1/4 lb.) hamburger. It's a shame they no longer produce it, because not enough customers were purchasing it. I hope they will bring it back to the market. Until then, I have the butcher grind for me eye of round. If you enjoy eating red meat and do not want to refrain, then I encourage you to make the switch to ground eye of round. You'll be doing your heart, health and waistline a lot of good!

The second time I break the rule is when I "choose to wander". Example: a small piece of chocolate. Remember, this is done very rarely!

(Just a note: I am not a big fan of fat-free cheeses or margarines, but in my recipes they taste good.)

Butter & Margarines

Butter Buds (found in spice or diet section)
Butter flavored Pam Spray
Cooking sprays (non-fat-off brands are fine)
I Can't Believe It's Not Butter Spray
Ultra Fat-Free Promise Margarine

Breads/Grains

Aunt Millie's Breads & Buns
Enriched Flour
Father Sam's Kangaroo Bread
Flour tortillas fat-free (Buena Vista is Good)
Graham crackers
Healthy Valley fat free cookies

♥♥♥♥♥♥♥♥♥♥♥♥♥♥♥♥♥♥♥♥♥♥♥♥♥

♥♥♥♥♥♥♥♥♥♥♥♥♥♥♥♥♥♥♥♥♥♥♥♥♥♥♥♥

Breads/Grains con't.

Healthy Valley Fat-Free Granola (I use for my homemade granola bars)
Italian seasoned bread crumbs
Lite breads (40 calories - no fat per slice) (Aunt Millie's, Bunny & Wonder are good)
Oyster crackers
Pastas (all except egg noodles)
Pillsbury Buttermilk Biscuits
Pillsbury Pizza Crust
Quaker brand Rice Cakes (caramel & strawberry flavored)
Quick cooking oats
Rice (whole grain enriched)
Rightshape Biscuits (buttermilk flavor)
Vegetable bread
Whole grain & white rice
Whole wheat flour

Beverages

Bottled water (don't be fooled by flavored waters; a lot of them are loaded with sugar & calories)
Cider
Country Time Lemonade (sugar free)
Crystal Light (sugar free)
Dole Fruit Juices (100%)
Grapefruit Juice (100%)
Kool-Aid (sugar free)
Orange Juice (100%)
Prune Juice (100%)
Tea (instant or tea bag)
Tomato Juice
V-8 Juice
Virgin Mary Juice

Cheese

(To be honest with you, I do not like fat-free cheese, but used properly in recipes they can taste delicious!)

Blue Cheese
Healthy Choice brand fat free (My favorite brand)
Italian topping (grated)
Parmesan (grated)
Ricotta- Fat Free

Condiments

Almond extract
Braum's fat free fudge topping
Coconut extract
Cornstarch
Dressings (fat-free)

Condiments con't.

Equal
Evaporated skim milk (lite)
Hidden Valley Reduced Calorie Dry Salad Dressing Mix
Honey
Karo Syrup
Kraft Free Mayonnaise & Miracle Whip
Kroger brand fat free ice cream toppings
Liquid smoke
*Lite syrups (I like Mrs. Butterworths)
Mint extract
Mrs. Richardson's fat free ice cream toppings
Mustard
Not So Sloppy Joe Mix
Nutra-Sweet
*Pam spray (non fat cooking spray)
Preserves & jellies (low sugar)
Smuckers fat free toppings
Soy sauce (Lite)
Taco seasoning mix
Teriyaki Marinade (Lite)
Tomato Sauce
Vanilla
*The off brand of these items are less expensive and good

Dairy

Buttermilk (non-fat)
Cottage cheese - non-fat (I like all of them)
Dry Powdered milk non-fat (use in recipes -I don't care to drink it)
Evaporated skim milk
Flavorite brand fat-free yogurts & non-fat cottage cheese
Frozen yogurt (be careful, some are loaded with calories because of high sugar content!)
Skim milk
Sour cream - fat-free (Land-O-Lakes, Light & Lively)
Yogurts - fat-free (watch labels-high sugar content means high calorie count)

Fruits and Veggies

Applesauce
Canned vegetables - no salt added
Canned fruits in fruit juice only (no heavy syrups)
All fresh vegetables except for avocado - Major Fat!!

♥♥♥♥♥♥♥♥♥♥♥♥♥♥♥♥♥♥♥♥♥♥♥♥♥♥♥♥

Fruits and Veggies con't.

All frozen vegetables and fruits with no sugar added
Cranberry sauce
Lite Fruit Cocktail
Pie fillings - lite - cherry, blueberry, apple (The off brand pie fillings taste fine.)
Hot Chili Beans - I like Brook's brand

Junk Food

(Usually no fat, but still too much sugar or salt to eat a lot of.)

Caramel corn (most brands are only 1 gram fat but high in sugar content)
Entenmanns Fat-Free Baked Goods
Frito Lays Potato Crisp (new-potato chip substitute) They're delicious - if you like Pringles you'll like these! Only 1.5 gr. fat per 100 calories (about 12 chips)
Frozen fat-free yogurts
Hostess "Lite" Twinkies & Brownies (It's hard to believe they're really low fat.)
Jello brand fat-free pudding & pudding cups
Keebler Elfin Delights
Little Debbie's Lite Oatmeal Pies & Brownies (new)
Marshmallows
Pepperidge Farm Fat-Free Brownies & Blondies (too good!)
Pretzels
Pop Chips (by Betty Crocker)
Rice Cakes (Quaker strawberry & caramel flavored)
Skinnies Corn Chips (These are hard to find; here's their number— 813-278-0244)
Smart Pop microwave popcorn by Orville Redenbacher
Snackwells cookies

Meats, Fish, Poultry

Beef (Eye of Round, London Broil, Flank Steak, Top Loin)
Canadian bacon
Chicken breast (no skin - dark meat has twice as much fat!)
Crabmeat (imitation) flake or stick
Fish (the white ones are lower in fats, *i.e.* Flounder, Grouper, Pike, Sole, Cod, Orange Roughy, Monk Fish, Perch, Scallops)

Meats, Fish, Poultry con't.

Hot dogs - Healthy Choice (1 gr. fat), Hormel light & lean (1 gr. fat) Oscar Mayer Fat-Free
Shell Fish (Lobster, Crab, Shrimp)
Tuna (packed in water)
Turkey Breast (no skin-dark meat has twice as much fat!)

Other Items

Dream Whip
Eggs (use only the whites)
Egg Beaters
Lite Cool Whip
Pasta

Pre-Packaged Items

Applesauce
Betty Crocker "Lite" Cake, Brownie, Bread & Muffin Mixes
Boullion Cubes (Chicken, Beef, and Vegetable flavors)
Campbell's Healthy Request low fat and fat-free soups and sauces
Gold Medal Fudge Brownie Mix
Health Valley Chili and Soups
Healthy Choice Soups and Sauces (low and no -fat)
Heinz Homestyle Gravy - Lite
Instant Mashed Potatoes
Jiffy Cake Mixes
Legumes (Beans - canned or dry variety & lentils)
Martha White's Lite Mixes (Muffin, etc.)
Old El Paso fat-free refried beans
Pancake & Buttermilk Pancake Mix
Pasta
Pillsbury Lovin' Lites Brownie, Cake & Muffin Mixes
Pillsbury Lovin' Lites Frostings
Special K Fat-Free Waffles
Spaghetti O's
Stuffin Mixes (Stove Top) look for brands that have only 2 gr. fat per serving as packaged

Sauces

Healthy Choice Spaghetti Sauce
Heinz Homestyle Lite Gravies (in a jar)
Pepperidge Farm Stroganoff Gravy
Prego Spaghetti and Pizza Sauces (Lite Ones)
Ragu Pizza Quick Sauce
Ragu Today's Recipe Spaghetti Sauces (low fat)

FAST & EASY

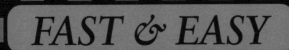

DOWN HOME COOKIN' WITHOUT THE DOWN HOME FAT

Section 1

♥♥♥♥♥♥♥♥♥♥♥♥♥♥♥♥♥♥♥♥♥♥♥♥♥

*Write your personal notes and
names of favorite recipes here.*

Appetizers
Snacks
Beverages

♥♥♥♥♥♥♥♥♥♥♥♥♥♥♥♥♥♥♥♥♥♥♥♥♥

Mini Contents

(Appetizers, Snacks, Beverages)

♥♥♥♥♥♥♥♥♥♥♥♥♥♥♥♥♥♥♥♥♥♥♥♥♥

♥♥♥♥♥♥♥♥♥♥♥♥♥♥♥♥♥♥♥♥♥♥♥♥♥♥♥♥♥

♥ "Seconds Please" Mexican Dip ♥

It doesn't get any easier than this! (or tastier).
Eat as a meal or appetizer.

- 1 - 16 oz. jar of mild thick 'n chunky picante or thick chunky salsa (I use "Old El Paso" brand picante)
- 1 - 16 oz. can vegetarian refried beans (I use "Old El Paso")
- 1 - 16 oz. ground eye of round (beef)
- 1 - 8 oz. pkg. no-fat Mexican cheese (I use Healthy Choice brand)

In large pan brown beef. (Do not drain juices) Add cheese, picante and refried beans, stir until well mixed and heated. Keep warm in a crock pot. Serve warm with low-fat tortilla chips! MMM! MMM! GOOD!

Yield: 15 - ¼ lb. servings   Calories: 87 per serving
Fat: 1.43 grams(not including chips)

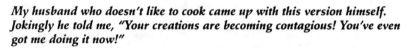

♥ Italian Dip ♥

Great for baked Tostidos or pretzels.

My husband who doesn't like to cook came up with this version himself. Jokingly he told me, "Your creations are becoming contagious! You've even got me doing it now!"

- 14 oz. Ragu Pizza Sauce (We like garlic and basil flavor.)
- 16 oz. fat-free sour cream
- 8 oz. fancy shredded mozzarella cheese (Healthy Choice brand)

Mix together. Serve chilled.

Yield: 19-2 oz. servings   Calories: 56   Fat: .5 grams

♥♥♥♥♥♥♥♥♥♥♥♥♥♥♥♥♥♥♥♥♥♥♥♥♥♥♥♥♥

♥♥♥♥♥♥♥♥♥♥♥♥♥♥♥♥♥♥♥♥♥♥♥♥♥♥♥♥

♥ *Mexican Confetti Dip* ♥

This is a great source of protein.
I like to eat this for lunch.

1 (12 oz.) can whole kernel corn - drained
1 (15.5 oz.) can black beans - drained
$^1/_3$ cup fat-free Italian Salad Dressing (I use Marzetti brand)
1 (16 oz.) jar of your favorite chunky salsa.

Mix all together. Chill. Presto! You're done!

Serve with Baked Tostito Chips

Other ways to use this recipe:
—Warm a flour tortilla in microwave. Fill center with $^1/_4$ cup of dip. Fold up as you would a burrito.
—Toss $^1/_2$ cup with $1^1/_2$ cup of your favorite lettuces for a tasty twist to your salad!

Yield: 6 servings (approx. 8 oz. each serving)
Calories: 78 per serving   Fat: .75 gram per serving

♥ *Fruit Flavored Cream Cheese Spreads* ♥

Great for bagels or crackers!

The high fat in those so called "lite" expensive flavored cheese spreads got my creativity going! I'm so pleased with these! They all taste absolutely delicious and not 1 gram of fat!

2-8 oz. packages of Healthy Choice fat-free cream cheese
$^1/_2$ cup your favorite brand jam. (If it's not sweet enough add 1 or 2 envelopes Nutra-Sweet.)

Here are my favorite type of jams to use in this recipe

—strawberry   —blackberry
—blueberry   —raspberry
—apricot   —peach

Serving size: 2 tablespoons

Yield: 20 servings   Calories: 40   Fat: 0 grams

ALL LANGUAGES UNDERSTAND THE COMMUNICATION
OF A SMILE.

♥♥♥♥♥♥♥♥♥♥♥♥♥♥♥♥♥♥♥♥♥♥♥♥♥♥

♥♥♥♥♥♥♥♥♥♥♥♥♥♥♥♥♥♥♥♥♥♥♥♥♥♥♥♥

♥ *No Cooking Mexican Dip* ♥

Layer in this order - follow the numbers:

Kids Cookin'

#1 - 8 oz. no-fat cream cheese (I use Healthy Choice)
    beaten with 8 oz. fat-free sour cream
#2 - 16 oz. your favorite thick and chunky salsa
    (picante or taco sauce may be used if desired)
#3 - 2 or 3 green onions, chopped
#4 - 1½ cup thinly sliced lettuce
#5 - 1 medium tomato diced
#6 - 8 oz. Healthy Choice fat-free Mexican Shredded
    Cheese or fat-free shredded cheddar cheese
1 bag of low fat tortilla chips

Beat cream cheese and sour cream together. Spread on cake
plate. Layer other ingredients on top of cream mixture in exact
order as listed above. Set tortilla chips in a bowl and serve.

Without Chips—   Yield: 15 servings (3 oz. each)
                      Calories: 60   Fat: 0.1 grams

♥ *"Chili Cheeser Pleaser" Dip* ♥

It's hard to believe it's only 1 gram of fat!

2 - 15 oz. cans of Healthy Valley Fat-Free Chili with
    black beans (spicy vegetarian)
1 lb. ground eye of round (beef)
8 oz. Healthy Choice fat-free fancy shredded cheddar
    cheese

Brown hamburger. Add both cans of chili and 8 oz. of cheddar
cheese. Mix well over medium-low heat, until cheese is
melted.

Serve warm with either low-fat tortilla chips, fat-free pretzel
chips or low-fat bugles.

Yield: 15-3 oz. servings   Calories: 84   Fat: 1.06 grams
Serving information is for dip only. Snacks not included.

WE SHOULD CELEBRATE WEDDING ANNIVERSARIES
MORE DILIGENTLY THAN BIRTHDAYS, BECAUSE
BIRTHDAYS COME WHETHER YOU WANT THEM TO OR
NOT, BUT WEDDING ANNIVERSARIES YOU HAVE TO
WORK AT ACHIEVING.

♥♥♥♥♥♥♥♥♥♥♥♥♥♥♥♥♥♥♥♥♥♥♥♥♥♥♥

♥♥♥♥♥♥♥♥♥♥♥♥♥♥♥♥♥♥♥♥♥♥♥♥♥♥♥♥

♥ *Cool & Creamy Spicy Tortilla Dip* ♥

Kids Cookin'

I created this recipe especially for Oprah as a gift when I was fortunate to be in her studio audience. (By the way she is even more beautiful in person!) She was so kind; she even sent me a thank you note!

16 oz. fat-free sour cream
16 oz. jar of your favorite chunky salsa

For a heartier dip add 8 oz. fancy shredded fat-free cheddar cheese. (I like Healthy Choice brand.)

Mix together, and refrigerate. Serve with low-fat tortilla chips, or any other of your favorite snacks as a dip. (Like low-fat "Bugles".)

Note: If you like spicier foods, feel free to add a few drops of Tabasco sauce.

I like to use a chunky salsa rather than a regular salsa.

Yield: 30-2 Tbs. servings   Calories: 10   Fat: 0 grams

Kids Cookin'

♥ *Cool & Creamy Salsa Salad Dressing* ♥

16 oz. fat-free sour cream
16 oz. jar of your favorite salsa or taco sauce
$1/3$ - $1/2$ cup skim milk
Tabasco Sauce to taste (if desired)

Mix all ingredients well. Serve chilled. Keep refrigerated.

If you like a thinner-runnier salad dressing just add more skim milk.

Yield: 34-2 Tbs. servings   Calories: 10   Fat: 0 grams

♥♥♥♥♥♥♥♥♥♥♥♥♥♥♥♥♥♥♥♥♥♥♥♥♥♥♥♥

♥♥♥♥♥♥♥♥♥♥♥♥♥♥♥♥♥♥♥♥♥♥♥♥♥♥♥♥♥

♥ *Fat-Free Vegetable Dip* ♥   *Kids Cookin'*

1 pkg. reduced calorie Hidden Valley Ranch Salad
   Dressing mix - dry
1 packet Equal® (OR 2 tsp. sugar)
3/4 cup no-fat cottage cheese
4 oz. fat-free cream cheese
3/4 cup no-fat sour cream
3 Tbs. water

Beat cottage cheese on high for 1-2 minutes. (Until smooth and creamy) Add everything else. Beat on medium until well blended.

Yield: 8 servings   With Equal: Calories: 35   Fat: 0 grams
                    With Sugar: Calories: 39   Fat: 0 grams

♥ *Creamy Blue Cheese Salad Dressing* ♥
If you like blue cheese, you'll love this!!

1/4 cup skim milk
1 cup fat-free sour cream (I use Land-O-Lakes brand)
1 cup fat-free mayonnaise (I use Kraft free)
1/4 cup blue cheese (I use Sargento's - natural crumbled
   2 oz.)

Mix and cover. Refrigerate for at least 24 hours before using. The refrigeration time allows for the cheese to flavor the dressing.

Kids Cookin'

♥ *Ham & Cheese Spread* (for fat-free crackers) ♥

8 oz. fat-free cream cheese (I use Healthy Choice)
1/2 medium red onion (about 1/2 cup)
2 - 6 oz. packages deli-thin sliced ham

Put all ingredients in food processor at once. Keep on for about 35-45 seconds. Put into container and place in the middle of fat-free crackers. (Make ahead and keep refrigerated - wrapped). Don't put fat-free crackers around dip until ready to serve..

Yield: 32 - 1 Tbs. servings
Calories: 18   Fat: .62 grams (not including crackers)

♥♥♥♥♥♥♥♥♥♥♥♥♥♥♥♥♥♥♥♥♥♥♥♥♥♥♥♥♥

♥♥♥♥♥♥♥♥♥♥♥♥♥♥♥♥♥♥♥♥♥♥♥♥♥

♥ *Shrimp Cocktail Spread* ♥

8 oz. fat-free cream cheese (I use Kraft Philadelphia
   "Free")
1 cup cocktail sauce (use your favorite brand or make
   your own with ketchup and horseradish)
1 box of your favorite fat-free crackers - I like
   Snackwell's and also Health Valley brands.
1½ cup Salad Shrimp (frozen) - cooked as directed on
   package and drained of any juices

Using a serving plate or cake plate (about 12" across) with
knife spread cream cheese within ½ inches from rim of plate,
covering the bottom of the plate completely. Spread cocktail
sauce over cream cheese. Place shrimp on top of cocktail
sauce. Serve with your favorite fat-free crackers.

Yield: 12 servings   Calories: 59 w/o crackers
                       Fat: .41 grams

♥ *Ham & Cheese Ball* ♥

4 oz. Healthy Choice ham or turkey ham - very thinly
   chopped
2 - 8 oz. fat-free cream cheese
4 green onions - chopped
4 oz. can mushroom pieces - chopped (water drained)
1 Tbs. mustard

Set ½ of the chopped ham aside. Mix all remaining ingredients
together well. Roll into a ball. Press remaining ham onto ball
covering entire ball surface.

Chill. Serve with fat-free crackers. (I like Snackwell's brand).

Yield: 12 servings (2 oz. each)   Calories: 57
              Fat: 0.4 grams

LIFE IS SHORT, SO MAKE IT SWEET.

♥♥♥♥♥♥♥♥♥♥♥♥♥♥♥♥♥♥♥♥♥♥♥♥♥

♥♥♥♥♥♥♥♥♥♥♥♥♥♥♥♥♥♥♥♥♥♥♥♥♥♥♥♥

♥ *South of the Border Cheese Spread* ♥

8 oz. fat-free cream cheese - softened
16 oz. fat-free sour cream
16 oz. jar of your favorite salsa
16 oz. fat-free shredded cheddar or taco cheese

With blender, mix ingredients thoroughly.

Serve chilled with crackers. (I like Snackwell's fat-free brand)
or low-fat tortilla chips.

Yield: 28 servings (2 oz. each)   Calories: 45
                          Fat: 0 grams

♥ *Caesar Oyster Crackers* ♥

*My husband loves to snack on junk food snacks! My problem with that,
even though he's slender, is that he's eating loads of fat. So I try to keep as
little of high fat munchie type snacks around as I can. To satisfy his
"Munchies Tooth" I've created some very low fat, crunchy and tasty
snacks. I really like this one! He does, too!*

11 oz. oyster crackers
1 - 1.2 oz. envelope gourmet Caesar Salad Dressing
      mix (Good Seasons)
non-fat cooking spray

Put in either a Zip-loc bag or a container with an airtight seal
73 of the oyster crackers. Quickly spray with non-fat cooking
spray. Sprinkle with $^1/_3$ of the dry salad dressing mix. Repeat
this process 2 times more. Shake well before eating to insure
good coverage of the seasonings.

Yield: 21 servings (16 crackers each)   Calories: 67
                          Fat: 1 gram

(*Note - If you are able to buy "fat-free" oyster crackers, this
recipe would be fat-free also.)

♥♥♥♥♥♥♥♥♥♥♥♥♥♥♥♥♥♥♥♥♥♥♥♥♥♥♥♥

♥♥♥♥♥♥♥♥♥♥♥♥♥♥♥♥♥♥♥♥♥♥♥♥♥♥♥

♥ *Zesty Snack Mix* ♥

1 pkg. Hidden Valley Reduced Calorie Original Ranch
    Salad Dressing mix - dry. (Do not add anything to
    it.) 1.1 oz. size
9 cups Kellogg's Crispix cereal
non-fat cooking spray

Pour Crispix cereal onto cookie sheets. Spray Crispix cereal
with a non-fat cooking spray. Sprinkle dry salad dressing mix
over cereal immediately. The cooking spray will hold the
seasoning onto the cereal. Pour into a large plastic bag and
shake. Store at room temperature.

If this is too zesty for you just add more Crispix cereal.

Yield: 9-1 cup servings   Calories: 126   Fat: 0 grams

♥ *Sweet & Salty Snack Mix* ♥

8 cups Ripple Crisp Honey Bran cereal
8 cups fat-free pretzels (broken up into 1/2" -1" pieces.
    Just break them with your hands)
2 cups raisins

Mix all together by hand. Store at room temperature in
airtight container. Stays crisp!

A huge hit for the kids! (And healthy too!) No cooking
involved. Great for kids to make and eat. You know kids
always like food more when they help make it!

Yield: 25 servings (approx. 1 cup each)   Calories: 105
              Fat: 0.7 grams

♥♥♥♥♥♥♥♥♥♥♥♥♥♥♥♥♥♥♥♥♥♥♥♥♥♥♥

♥♥♥♥♥♥♥♥♥♥♥♥♥♥♥♥♥♥♥♥♥♥♥♥♥♥♥

♥ Bar-B-Que Snack Mix ♥ *Kids Cookin'*

9 cups Kellogg's Crispix cereal
1 packet (1.9 oz.) Barbecue Chicken Seasoned Coating
    microwave mix
no-fat cooking spray

Cover cookie sheet with foil. Put 3 cups of Crispix cereal on
foil. Spray with non-fat cooking spray. Sprinkle with barbecue
seasoning mix. Put into airtight container. Repeat this process
until all 9 cups of Crispix cereal are coated. Once all of the
seasoned cereal is in an airtight container, shake the container
to help cover cereal with more seasoning.

Presto!! You're done!!

Yield: 9-1 cup servings   Calories: 132   Fat: .44 grams

♥ Homemade Berry Wine Cooler ♥

1 - 25.4 oz. bottle of "Boons" brand Snow Creek Berry
    flavored apple wine product
2 cups diet cherry Seven-Up
1 - 40 oz. bottle of Dole 100% Juice Country
    Raspberry

Pour all ingredients into a 2 quart pitcher. Chill. Serve chilled.

Yield: 10 servings (8 oz. each)   Calories: 105
              Fat: 0 grams

♥ Cranberry Cooler (Slushy Drink) ♥

Kids Cookin'

4 - 4½ cups ice
½ cup whole berry cranberry sauce
3 cups cranberry breeze flavored crystal light drink
    (prepare as directed on can)
4 packets Equal® (OR 3 Tbs. sugar)

Put everything in blender on high, mix for 30-45 seconds.
Serve immediately.

Yield: 5 servings   With Equal: Calories: 15   Fat: 0 grams
              With Sugar: Calories: 39   Fat: 0 grams

♥♥♥♥♥♥♥♥♥♥♥♥♥♥♥♥♥♥♥♥♥♥♥♥♥♥♥

♥♥♥♥♥♥♥♥♥♥♥♥♥♥♥♥♥♥♥♥♥♥♥♥♥♥♥

♥ *Cheese Ball* (Makes Two) ♥

1 pkg. Hidden Valley Ranch Reduced Calorie Salad
    Dressing mix
1 lb. Healthy Choice fat-free fancy shredded cheddar
    cheese
12 oz. fat-free cream cheese - softened (I use Healthy
    Choice brand)
1/2 cup fat-free mayonnaise (Do not use Miracle Whip!!!)
1/2 cup skim milk

Mix Ranch dressing with mayonnaise and milk. Mix softened
cream cheese with dressing mixture until thoroughly blended.
Add cheddar cheese and mix well.

Form into two balls. Refrigerate overnight, or at least a couple
of hours.

Yield: 18 servings (2 oz. each)   Calories: 57
                    Fat: 0 grams

♥ *Chipped Beef Cheese Ball* ♥

3 - 8 oz. fat-free cream cheese
1 1/2 - 2 tsp. liquid smoke (depending on how smoky you
    like it)
2 - 2.5 oz. size chipped beef - chopped (I use Carl Budding
    beef)
1 small onion chopped (approximately 1/2 cup)

Mix all ingredients well with blender. With hands, shape into
a ball. Garnish with fresh parsley if desired.

Serve with fat-free crackers.

For a quick chipped beef cheese spread - everything exactly
the same, but put into food processor for about 1 1/2 - 2
minutes. Pour into bowl and garnish with crackers.

Yield: 16 servings (2 oz. each)   Calories: 45
                                          Fat: 0.6 grams

♥♥♥♥♥♥♥♥♥♥♥♥♥♥♥♥♥♥♥♥♥♥♥♥♥♥

♥♥♥♥♥♥♥♥♥♥♥♥♥♥♥♥♥♥♥♥♥♥♥♥

♥ *Country Raspberry Tea* ♥ *Kids Cookin'*

3 tsp. instant tea to 1 quart cold water
½ quart Country Raspberry 100% juice (by Dole)
3 Tbs. Nutra-Sweet® Spoonful™ (OR 3 Tbs. sugar)

Mix all ingredients together. Serve chilled.

Yield: 6 (8 oz.) servings
With Nutra-Sweet®: Calories: 47 per serving   Fat: 0 grams
With sugar: Calories: 71 per serving   Fat: 0 grams

♥ *Mandarin Tangerine Tea* ♥

Kids Cookin'

3 tsp. instant tea to 1 quart cold water
1 quart Mandarin Tangerine 100% juice (by Dole)
2 Tbs. Nutra-Sweet® Spoonful™ (OR 2 Tbs. sugar)

Mix all ingredients together. Serve chilled.

Yield: 8 (8 oz.) servings
With Nutra-Sweet®: Calories: 80   Fat: 0 grams
With sugar: Calories: 96   Fat: 0 grams

Kids Cookin'

♥ *Cherry Tea* ♥

These imitation flavored teas can save you oodles of money! Save your name brand single serving size tea bottles and refill with your own homemade! Now that's recycling!

1 quart tea - 3 tsp. instant tea to 1 quart water
½ quart Mountain Cherry 100% Juice by Dole
1 Tbs. Nutra-Sweet® Spoonful™ (OR 1 Tbs. sugar)

Mix all ingredients together. Serve chilled.

Yield: 6 servings (8 oz. each)
With Nutra-Sweet®: Calories: 40 per serving   Fat: 0 grams
With sugar: Calories 48 per serving   Fat: 0 grams

♥♥♥♥♥♥♥♥♥♥♥♥♥♥♥♥♥♥♥♥♥♥♥♥

Kids Cookin' ❤ *Banana Berry Slushy* ❤

1 banana
1 cup black raspberries or blackberries
$^1/_2$ cup Nutra-Sweet® Spoonful™ (OR $^1/_2$ cup sugar)
3 cups ice
2 cups water
1 - 0.13 envelope black cherry Kool-Aid

Put everything in blender on high, mix for 30-45 seconds.
Serve immediately.

Yield: 5 servings
      Nutra-Sweet® Spoonful™: Calories: 71   Fat: 0.2 grams
      With Sugar: Calories: 110   Fat: 0. 2 grams

Kids Cookin' ❤ *Cherry Slushies* ❤

12 Bing cherries - with seeds taken out
4 cups ice
$^1/_2$ tsp. cherry flavored sugar-free Kool-Aid
$2^1/_2$ cups cold water
$^1/_2$ cup sugar or 7-8 packets Equal

Put everything in blender on "mix" or "ice crush" setting.
Leave on for 30-45 seconds. Pour into glasses.

Yield: 5-8 oz. servings   Calories: 89   Fat: 0 grams

Kids Cookin' ❤ *Warm Whatcha'Macallit* ❤

1 gallon cider
2 liter diet Ginger Ale
$^1/_2$ cup red hots (little red cinnamons)
cinnamon sticks (optional)

Warm on medium heat until warm. Approximately 7-10
minutes. Serve warm with cinnamon stick.

Yield: 24 servings   Calories: 88   Fat: 0 grams

**THINK OF HOW YOU WANT TO BE REMEMBERED IN
10 YEARS WHEN YOU LOOK BACK AT YOUR PAST.
LIVE IT NOW.**

♥♥♥♥♥♥♥♥♥♥♥♥♥♥♥♥♥♥♥♥♥♥♥♥♥♥♥♥♥♥

♥ *Fruit Punch* ♥

2 - 2 quarts cherry sugar-free Kool-Aid - prepared
1 - 2 liter diet cherry Seven-Up
2 - 12 oz. cans of frozen orange juice - prepared

Mix and serve chilled.

For a lower calorie punch use only 1 can (12 oz.) orange juice.
I like it just as well as 2 cans, and it's not as fattening.

If using a punch bowl, slice 1 orange into slices with rind on.
For decorating, allow slices to float on top of punch.

Made with 2 cans Orange Juice
Yield: 36 servings (8 oz. each)   Calories: 14   Fat: 0 grams

Made with 1 can Orange Juice
Yield: 30 servings   Calories: 11   Fat: 0 grams

♥ *Orange Slushy* ♥

4½ cups ice
½ tsp. orange sugar-free Kool-Aid
2½ cups cold water
7 - 8 packets Equal® (OR ⅓ cup sugar)
11 oz. can Mandarin oranges with light syrup

Fill a 5 cup blender with all ingredients. Blend for 30-45
seconds. Pour into glasses and serve.

Yield: 5 servings   With Equal®: Calories: 37   Fat: 0.1 grams
                         With Sugar: Calories: 64   Fat: 0.1 grams

♥♥♥♥♥♥♥♥♥♥♥♥♥♥♥♥♥♥♥♥♥♥♥♥♥♥♥♥♥♥

♥♥♥♥♥♥♥♥♥♥♥♥♥♥♥♥♥♥♥♥♥♥♥♥♥♥♥

♥ *Peach Tea* ♥

3 tsp. instant tea to 1 quart cold water
½ quart Orchard Peach 100% juice (by Dole)
2½ Tbs. Nutra-Sweet (<u>OR</u> 2½ Tbs. sugar)

Mix all ingredients together. Serve chilled.

Yield: 6 (8 oz.) servings
Nutra-Sweet®: Calories: 47   Fat: 0 grams
With Sugar: Calories 67   Fat: 0 grams

♥ *Very Berry Tea* ♥

3 tsp. instant tea with 1 quart cold water
½ quart Cranberry/Strawberry Juice Cocktail Blend
     with Grape Juice
8 oz. Mountain Cherry 100% juice (by Dole)
8 oz. Country Raspberry 100% juice (by Dole)
3 Tbs. Nutra-Sweet (<u>OR</u> 3 Tbs. sugar)

Mix all ingredients together. Serve chilled.

With Nutra Sweet®: Calories: 47   Fats: 0 grams
With Sugar: Calories: 71   Fats: 0 grams

♥ *Hawaiian Slushy Drink* ♥

1 - 15 oz. can pineapple in its own juices
2 bananas
⅓ cup Nutra-Sweet® Spoonful™ (<u>OR</u> ½ cup sugar)
between 2 and 2½ cups ice (it depends on how icy you
     like it.)
1 tsp. of pina-pineapple flavor sugar-free Kool-Aid

Fill blender to top with water. Put everything in a blender. Mix
on high for 30-45 seconds.

Yield: 6 cups
With: Nutra-Sweet® Spoonful™: Calories: 92   Fat: 0.1 grams
With sugar: Calories: 156   Fat: 0.1 grams

♥♥♥♥♥♥♥♥♥♥♥♥♥♥♥♥♥♥♥♥♥♥♥♥♥♥♥

♥♥♥♥♥♥♥♥♥♥♥♥♥♥♥♥♥♥♥♥♥♥♥♥♥♥♥

♥ *Banana Smoothie* ♥

1 banana
1¹/₂ cups skim milk
5 Tbs. Nutra-Sweet® Spoonful™ (OR 5 Tbs. sugar)
2 cups ice

Put everything in blender on high, mix for 30-45 seconds.
Serve immediately.

Yield: 5 servings
  With Nutra-Sweet® Spoonful™: Calories: 47   Fat: 0.1 grams
  With sugar: Calories: 93   Fat: 0.1 grams

♥ *Mint Tea* ♥

If you like "Snapple" brand of mint tea, you'll love this, and it'll save you loads of money!

2 quarts of hot water
8 tea bags (your favorite brand)
2 drops mint extract (found in seasoning section of store)
Sugar to taste — optional

Put tea bags in hot water. Let stand overnight.

Remove tea bags. Put 2 drops of mint extract into tea.

Serve in tall glasses with ice.

Yield: 8 Serving   Calories: 6   Fat: 0 grams

ONE CAN NOT LIVE ON COD LIVER OIL ALONE.

♥♥♥♥♥♥♥♥♥♥♥♥♥♥♥♥♥♥♥♥♥♥♥♥♥♥♥

Breads
Rolls
Muffins

♥♥♥♥♥♥♥♥♥♥♥♥♥♥♥♥♥♥♥♥♥♥♥♥♥♥♥♥

Mini Contents

(Breads, Rolls, Muffins)

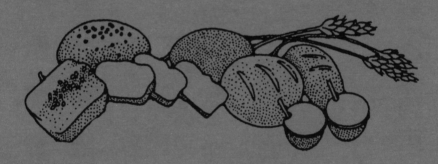

**WHEN YOUR PERSONALITY STARTS GETTING UGLY, YOU
KNOW IT'S TIME FOR SOME BEAUTY SLEEP!**

♥♥♥♥♥♥♥♥♥♥♥♥♥♥♥♥♥♥♥♥♥♥♥♥♥♥♥♥

♥ *Garlic Crisp* ♥

Pita bread (I use Father Sam's brand large size)
non-fat cooking spray
garlic salt
dried basil
grated Italian topping or grated Parmesan cheese - 1
    Tbs. per pita

Cut Pita bread in half then cut into quarters. (There will be 8 pieces for each Pita.)

Spray cut pieces of Pita, with non-fat spray. Sprinkle with garlic salt, grated Italian topping (or grated Parmesan cheese) and dried basil in that order.

Bake 350 degrees for 10 minutes or until slightly brown on edges.

Great warm or serve later w/salad instead of croutons.

Yield: 1 large size pita: 4 servings of 2 small quarters
                    Calories: 47   Fat: 0.6 grams

♥ *Cheesie Vegetable Bread* ♥

1 loaf of store bought vegetable bread-sliced thick
    ($^3/_4$") (find in deli area)
$^1/_2$ cup liquid Butter Buds
1 tsp. garlic salt
1 tsp. basil - dried
1 tsp. dried parsley
$^1/_4$ cup Parmesan cheese
2 Tbs. Molly McButter Cheese Sprinkles

Add garlic salt, dried basil and dried parsley to liquid Butter Buds. Spread liquid Butter Buds over thick sliced vegetable bread slices.

Spray cookie sheet with a non-fat spray. Lay slices of vegetable bread that has herb butter sauce spread on. Sprinkle with Molly McButter cheese and $^1/_4$ cup Parmesan cheese.

Put on top shelf in oven on broil until tops are browned and toasty. Serve warm. MMM!

Yield: 12 servings   Calories: 134   Fat: 2 grams

♥♥♥♥♥♥♥♥♥♥♥♥♥♥♥♥♥♥♥♥♥♥♥♥

♥ *Italian Biscuits* ♥

1 pkg. of 10 Rightshape Biscuits - Four Winds brand
   (Foodtown) <u>OR</u> Pillsbury Buttermilk Biscuits
4 Tbs. Progresso Bread Crumbs - Italian style

Spray cookie sheet with a non-fat spray. Preheat oven to 425
degrees. Gently press each biscuit into bread crumbs covering
the tops completely. With crumb side up place biscuits on
cookie sheet.

Bake 10 minutes at 425 degrees.

Tops will be golden brown. If desired you can warm 1 Tbs.
Butter Buds and brush tops of biscuits once cooked. Serve
warm.

Yield: 5 servings   No butter: Calories: 105   Fat: 1 gram

♥ *Sticky Bagels* (for breakfast) ♥

1 dozen bagels cut in half
8 oz. fat-free Ultra Promise Margarine
1/2 tsp. vanilla
2 tsp. cinnamon
1 cup brown sugar

Beat margarine, vanilla, brown sugar, and cinnamon for 1
minute on medium speed with blender.

Take bagel and dip top with spread just prepared. If needed
spread with knife. Broil at 450 degrees for 4-5 minutes, until
bubbly and brown. Serve warm.

Yield: 12 servings   Calories: 249   Fat: 1.2 grams
        24 servings   Calories: 124   Fat: 0.6 grams

♥♥♥♥♥♥♥♥♥♥♥♥♥♥♥♥♥♥♥♥♥♥♥♥

Soups
Salads
Vegetables

♥♥♥♥♥♥♥♥♥♥♥♥♥♥♥♥♥♥♥♥♥♥♥♥♥♥

Mini Contents

(Soups, Salads, Vegetables)

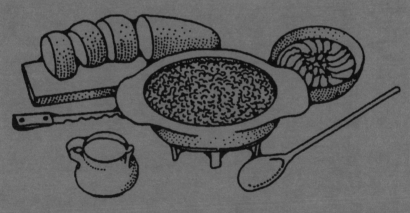

SOME THINGS ARE BETTER GIVEN AWAY — LOVE, HUGS AND SMILES.

♥♥♥♥♥♥♥♥♥♥♥♥♥♥♥♥♥♥♥♥♥♥♥♥♥♥

❤❤❤❤❤❤❤❤❤❤❤❤❤❤❤❤❤❤❤❤❤❤❤❤

❤ *Chicken Asparagus Soup* ❤

12 cups chicken broth
6 chicken breasts - skinless and boneless with fat
    removed
1 tsp. Cajun seasoning
3 bay leaves
1 pkg. (4.5 oz.) Staff brand rice & sauce cheddar
    broccoli mix
1 - 15 oz. can asparagus - cut into pieces
1 tsp. parsley
salt to taste - optional

Bring chicken broth to a rapid boil. Add chicken breast and all
ingredients. Bring to a rapid boil again. Reduce heat to a low
boil. Boil 10 minutes. Remove breasts and chop into bite size
pieces. Put cut-up breast pieces back into soup.

Serve warm. Remove bay leaves before eating.

Yield: 20 servings (1 cup each)   Calories: 116
              Fat: 1.8 grams

❤ *Vegetable Hobo Soup* ❤

I like to serve this vegetarian soup with warm vegetable bread.

3 lbs. frozen mixed vegetables
1 - 46 oz. can V-8 Vegetable Juice
2 bay leaves
salt and garlic powder to taste

Put all ingredients in a large soup pan or Dutch Oven. Bring to
a boil. Reduce heat. Cook 15 minutes. Serve hot.

Yield: 11 servings   Calories: 104   Fat: 0.8 grams

THERE IS ALWAYS HOPE.

❤❤❤❤❤❤❤❤❤❤❤❤❤❤❤❤❤❤❤❤❤❤❤

♥♥♥♥♥♥♥♥♥♥♥♥♥♥♥♥♥♥♥♥♥♥♥♥♥

 ♥ *Creamy Cucumbers* ♥

3 large cucumbers - peeled and sliced thinly
1 medium onion - sliced thinly
1 - 16 oz. bottle of Marzetti's fat-free Ranch Salad
    Dressing

Toss all above ingredients and chill. Serve chilled.

Yield: 14 servings (¹/₂ cup each)   Calories: 57
               Fat: 0.1 grams

Kids Cookin' ♥ *Tomato Zing Salad* ♥

Peel and slice thinly 2 large cucumbers
add 1 pint cherry tomatoes
cut and add 1 medium onion
make Seven Seas no-fat Italian dressing with rice
    vinegar
Toss vegetables in dressing.

Serve chilled.

Yield: 12 servings (¹/₂ cup each)   Calories: 17
               Fat: 0.2 grams

Kids Cookin'
♥ *Creamy Zucchini & Squash Salad* ♥

Peel and slice thinly:
    2 - 10" zucchini
    2 - 10" yellow squash
    Thinly slice 1 medium onion
    Toss with 16 oz. of Marzetti's Fat-Free Ranch Salad
        Dressing.

Serve chilled.

Yield: 15 servings (¹/₂ cup each)   Calories: 51
               Fat: 0.1 grams

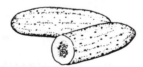

♥♥♥♥♥♥♥♥♥♥♥♥♥♥♥♥♥♥♥♥♥♥♥♥♥

♥♥♥♥♥♥♥♥♥♥♥♥♥♥♥♥♥♥♥♥♥♥♥♥♥♥♥

♥ Red-Wine Vinaigrette Cucumber Salad ♥

*A summer must! Great for cookouts! My children
and I like to nibble on these for a snack.*

Kids Cookin'

4 - 5 cucumbers, peeled and sliced into ¼" slices
1 - 16 oz. Seven-Seas Red-Wine Vinaigrette Salad
 Dressing

Mix above ingredients together. Chill.

Serve chilled.

Yield: 15 servings (½ cup each)   Calories: 13
                     Fat: 0.1 grams

♥ Papa Pasta Salad ♥

8 oz. uncooked Healthy Choice Smoked Sausage - cut
 into tiny pieces
16 oz. Rotini pasta
1 Tbs. + 1 tsp. Durkee Salad Seasoning
1½ cup fat-free Ranch Dressing (I use Henri's brand)

Cook Rotini pasta as directed on package. Drain. Rinse with
cold water until pasta is cool. Drain.

Combine all ingredients. Serve chilled.

Yield: 8 servings   Calories: 322   Fat: 2 grams

♥♥♥♥♥♥♥♥♥♥♥♥♥♥♥♥♥♥♥♥♥♥♥♥♥

♥♥♥♥♥♥♥♥♥♥♥♥♥♥♥♥♥♥♥♥♥♥♥♥♥

♥ *Summer Fiesta! Salad* ♥

For a faster salad, use store bought, already prepared, cup-up salad greens. (lettuce)

¹/₂ lb. cooked chicken breast or chicken breast lunch
    meat sliced into ¹/₄" strips
1 small onion chopped (red onion is best, but any one
    will do)
4 small hard boiled eggs (throw away yolks, use only
    the whites).
6 cups of your favorite lettuces (any combination is
    fine) torn into bite size pieces. (Iceburg, spinach &
    leaf are my favorites).
1 small carrot - diced
1 medium tomato cut into bite size pieces

Toss above ingredients together, in Honey Dijon Salad
Dressing.

Yield: 4 servings   Calories: 106 without dressing
                        Fat: 0.4 grams

Kids Cookin'

♥ *Hot-Not Fat-Fruit Salad* ♥

Note: If desired you can put all ingredients in a crockpot on low and let it simmer all day.
This is a soupy salad and needs to be served in a bowl. I like it as a dessert over frozen vanilla yogurt.

1 - 20 oz. can pineapple
1 - 20 oz. can pears
1 - 20 oz. can peaches
1 - 20 oz. can apricots
1 - 20 oz. can lite cherry pie filling
³/₄ cup brown sugar
1 lb. fat-free Ultra Promise Margarine

Drain fruit for at least 1 hour.

Mix brown sugar, margarine, fruit and pie filling together.

Bake at 350 degrees for 1 hour (or microwave on high till
warm about 5 minutes.)

Yield: 30 servings (¹/₂ cup each)   Calories: 69
                        Fat: 0.2 grams

♥♥♥♥♥♥♥♥♥♥♥♥♥♥♥♥♥♥♥♥♥♥♥♥♥

♥♥♥♥♥♥♥♥♥♥♥♥♥♥♥♥♥♥♥♥♥♥♥♥♥♥

♥ Fresh Broccoli Salad ♥ *Kids Cookin'*

$^1/_3$ cup Free Miracle Whip
$^1/_3$ cup Fat-Free Catalina Dressing OR Fat-Free Western
Dressing
1 large head fresh broccoli

Wash, clean and cut fresh broccoli into bite size pieces. Set
aside.

Combine Free Miracle Whip and Free Western Dressing (OR
Fat-Free Catalina). Mix well.
Pour dressing over broccoli. Stir until well coated with
dressing. Serve chilled.

♥ Apple Salad ♥

$1^1/_2$ cup no-fat cottage cheese
$^3/_4$ cup fat-free mayonnaise
$^1/_2$ cup Nutra-Sweet® Spoonful™ (OR $^1/_2$ cup sugar)
3 bananas sliced diagonally
4 cups apple - finely chopped (approximately 4-5 large
apples)
$^1/_4$ cup raisins - finely chopped
$^3/_4$ tsp. cinnamon

In blender, whip cottage cheese, mayonnaise, cinnamon and
Nutra-Sweet until cottage cheese is no longer lumpy, but
smooth and creamy. (About 3-4 minutes).

In medium bowl mix creamy mixture (you just prepared) with
chopped apples, raisins and sliced bananas. Presto! It's ready
to eat!

Yield: 16 servings ($^1/_2$ cup each)
With Nutra-Sweet® Spoonful™: Calories: 71 Fat: 0.2 grams
With sugar: Calories: 95   Fat: 0.2 grams

♥♥♥♥♥♥♥♥♥♥♥♥♥♥♥♥♥♥♥♥♥♥♥♥♥♥

❤❤❤❤❤❤❤❤❤❤❤❤❤❤❤❤❤❤❤❤❤❤❤❤❤❤❤❤

Kids Cookin'

❤ *Chicken Salad* ❤

Great for sandwiches on toasted lite bread or
stuffing in cherry tomatoes as appetizers!

2 tsp. sweet relish
3 tsp. Kraft Free No-fat Mayonnaise
1 pkg. Oscar Mayer Deli-thin Roasted Chicken Breast
    (6 oz. size) Cut into 1" pieces.

Put all ingredients in bowl. With blender mix together for
about 30 seconds. It doesn't get any easier than this!

Yield: 3 servings   Calories: 56   Fat: 2 grams

❤ *Mama's Beans* ❤

If you like green beans with ham you'll like this!

4 slices hardwood smoked white turkey lunchmeat -
    cut into tiny pieces
16 oz. frozen cut green beans
$^1/_3$ cup fat-free fancy shredded mozzarella cheese (I use
    Healthy Choice brand)
1 Tbs. grated Parmesan cheese
dash of pepper - optional
1 tsp. Molly McButter Garlic Butter Sprinkles (or any
    other fat-free brand of sprinkles) - optional

Mix green beans, mozzarella, cut up turkey and grated
parmesan cheese. Add seasonings if desired.

Microwave a total of 6-8 minutes, stirring occasionally. Serve
as a side dish or eat as a main meal.

Dish is completely cooked when beans are hot, crisp yet
tender, and cheese is melted.

Yield: 5 servings   Calories: 82   Fat: 2.1 grams

THIN MAY BE IN, BUT FIT
—NOT FAT—IS WHERE IT'S AT!

❤❤❤❤❤❤❤❤❤❤❤❤❤❤❤❤❤❤❤❤❤❤❤❤❤

♥♥♥♥♥♥♥♥♥♥♥♥♥♥♥♥♥♥♥♥♥♥♥♥

♥ *Apple Yam Casserole* ♥
This is a great dish for the holiday.

1 - 20 oz. can apple pie filling
1 - 24 oz. can yams
$^{1}/_{2}$ tsp. cinnamon
2 Tbs. brown sugar
dash of salt - optional

Drain juice from yams. Cut yams into bite sized pieces. Set aside. Cut apples in pie filling into bite size pieces. In a medium size bowl put apple pie filling, cinnamon, brown sugar and salt. Mix until well blended. Gently stir in cut-up yams.

Spray 2 quart casserole dish with no-fat cooking spray. Microwave until warm about 5 minutes, stirring occasionally.

Serve warm.

Yield: 12 servings   Calories: 121   Fat: 0.1 grams

♥ *Seasoned Rice* ♥
This dish is excellent with the "Oriental Teriyaki Beef Dinner".

1 cup long grain rice
$2^{1}/_{4}$ cups water
1 envelope Knorr vegetable soup mix (1.4 oz. size)

Spray saucepan with a non -fat cooking spray. In medium saucepan add all ingredients, stir and dissolve soup. Bring to a boil, reduce heat to simmering. Cover and cook approximately 20 minutes, covered.

Yield: 6 servings   Calories: 107   Fat: 0 grams

♥♥♥♥♥♥♥♥♥♥♥♥♥♥♥♥♥♥♥♥♥♥♥♥

♥♥♥♥♥♥♥♥♥♥♥♥♥♥♥♥♥♥♥♥♥♥♥♥♥♥♥

♥ *Oniony Chicken Rice Dish* ♥

1 lb. skinless, boneless raw chicken breast - cut into
    bite size pieces
1 - 14$^1/_2$ oz. can chicken broth (remove any floating
    fat)
2 cups frozen green beans
1 cup natural long grain rice
$^1/_4$ cup fat-free Ultra Promise Margarine
1 - 15 oz. pkg. onion soup mix - dry
$^1/_3$ cup water

Spray Dutch Oven with a non-fat cooking spray. Then put all
ingredients into the Dutch Oven over medium heat. Bring to a
boil. Reduce to simmer for 23 minutes covered. Stir
occasionally. Turn off heat and let stand for 5 minutes before
serving.

Yield: 6 servings   Calories: 255   Fat: 4 grams

♥ *Almost Homemade Dressing* ♥

The slight crunchiness of the corn mixed with the turkey, onion,
mushrooms and seasoning make this taste homemade—
to be honest—just as good as my homemade!

2 boxes chicken stuffing (Stove Top)
2 cups chopped turkey or chicken breast
1 - 16 oz. canned corn
1 medium onion chopped
1 pkg. Butter Buds
2 - 4 oz. cans sliced mushrooms
$^1/_8$ tsp. ground pepper
3$^1/_3$ cups water plus $^1/_2$ cup water

Put chopped onion, mushrooms, Butter Buds and seasoning
packets (from stuffing mixes) into medium saucepan over high
heat. Bring to a boil. Reduce heat. Add corn. Simmer 4
minutes. Add bread crumbs from stuffing boxes. Remove from
heat. Let sit 5 minutes. Heat turkey in microwave until warm
(about 40 seconds). Season turkey with pepper. Stir turkey
into stuffing. Serve immediately.

Yield: 12 servings

♥♥♥♥♥♥♥♥♥♥♥♥♥♥♥♥♥♥♥♥♥♥♥♥♥♥♥

♥ *Potatoes A-La-Larry* ♥

This delicious recipe is from a friend named Larry who is an excellent cook for the Cherry Street Mission, here in Toledo, Ohio. This recipe tastes so good, it can fool some folks into thinking they're made from scratch! Just between you and me, "Don't tell them they aren't unless they ask!" It'll be our little secret!

1 - 15 oz. - 20 oz. can potatoes-drained and mashed up
$\frac{1}{4}$ cup fresh onion-finely chopped (per every 8
    servings)
chicken broth (from a can preferably)
your favorite brand of instant mashed potatoes

Use skim milk and Fleishmann's Fat-Free Margarine

Substituting chicken broth for water use exact same measurement needed to prepare instant mashed potatoes, follow the boxed mashed potato recipe directions exactly. Bring chicken broth to a boil and stir into instant mashed potato flakes. Stir in milk, margarine, mashed potatoes and onion. Presto!! You are done.

Yield: $\frac{1}{3}$ cup serving size   Calories: 100
                     Fat: 0.5 grams

♥ *Green Bean Delite* ♥

3 - 15$\frac{1}{2}$ oz. French style green beans - drained
1 medium onion - chopped
8 oz. mushrooms - sliced thin
8 oz. lean ham - diced
$\frac{1}{2}$ cup liquid Butter Buds
3 Tbs. honey
1 tsp. lite salt (optional)

Saute onions and mushrooms in $\frac{1}{2}$ cup liquid Butter Buds until tender. Add ham, green beans, and honey. Cook over medium heat until heated thoroughly. Add salt if desired.

Yield: 15 servings ($\frac{1}{2}$ cup each)   Calories: 55
                     Fat: 0.9 grams

♥♥♥♥♥♥♥♥♥♥♥♥♥♥♥♥♥♥♥♥♥♥♥♥♥♥♥♥

♥ *Quick Asparagus Casserole* ♥

This is a nice variety to take to a potluck.

1 - 14½ oz. cans asparagus
1 envelope Butter Buds
2 Tbs. flour
2 cups non-fat buttermilk (skim milk can be substituted
    if desired)
½ cup light mozzarella cheese-shredded (I use
    Sargento Light)
½ Italian bread crumbs (I used Progresso brand)
(If you don't like the zest of the Italian you can use
    plain)

Spray a 9" x 13" pan with a non-fat cooking spray. Over low
heat warm milk, Butter Buds and flour in saucepan. Cook over
low heat, about 3 minutes, stirring constantly until thickened.
Add cheese and cook slowly on low heat 1 more minute.

Drain water from asparagus. Spread asparagus evenly in the 9"
x 13" pan. Pour sauce evenly over asparagus. Sprinkle bread
crumbs over entire dish.

Bake at 350 degrees for 15-20 minutes, until hot and bubbly.
Let cool a few minutes before serving.

Yield: 12 servings   Calories: 62   Fat: .83 grams

♥ *Buttered Collard Greens with Ham* ♥

1 apple cut into quarters with seeds taken out
2 Tbs. Butter Buds - dry
2 - 15 oz. cans chopped collard greens
6 oz. deli-thin sliced boiled ham - cut into bite size
    pieces (I use deli-thin Oscar Mayer boiled ham)
1 small onion - chopped (approx. ⅓ cup)

Drain collard greens. In large saucepan put in all ingredients,
over medium heat cover and bring to a boil. Reduce heat to
low. Simmer with lid on for 10 minutes. Remove apple
quarters before serving.

Yield: 6 servings   Calories: 60   Fat: 1.16 grams

YOU KNOW YOU'VE HAD TOO MUCH TO DRINK WHEN
YOUR EYEBALLS FEEL LIKE THEY'RE ABOUT TO FLOAT!

♥♥♥♥♥♥♥♥♥♥♥♥♥♥♥♥♥♥♥♥♥♥♥♥♥♥♥♥

Main Dishes & Casseroles

Mini Contents

(Main Dishes & Casseroles)

♥▼♥▼♥▼♥▼♥▼♥▼♥▼♥▼♥▼♥▼♥▼♥▼♥▼♥

♥ *Delicious Chicken Roll-Ups* ♥

1 pkg. Stove Top Stuffing Mix
1 pkg. Butter Buds
³/₄ cup chopped mushrooms
2 cups hot water
1 lb. roasted chicken breast lunchmeat slices

Combine 2 cups hot water, 1 pack of Butter Buds, mushrooms and seasoning packet from stuffing mix. Microwave on high for 2¹/₂ to 3 minutes. Add stuffing. Mix well. Cover tightly and let stand for 5 minutes.

Take each chicken breast lunchmeat slice and press about 2 Tbs. of stuffing mix in middle of lunchmeat slice. Bring sides of slice into middle and secure with toothpick.

Sauce:
    1 can of chicken broth
    ¹/₂ cup milk
    2 Tbs. cornstarch
    1 tsp. garlic salt
    ¹/₂ tsp. Jumbalaya Cajun Seasoning (optional)

Mix and add to broth. Heat until warm.

Lay chicken rolls on jelly roll pan (cookie sheet with edges) that has been sprayed with a non-fat cooking spray. Pour sauce over tops of each roll, allowing sauce to cover bottom of pan. Cover with foil. Bake at 350 degrees for 15 minutes.

Yield: 6 servings   Calories: 197   Fat: 2.2 grams

THANKFULNESS IS AN ATTITUDE WE CHOOSE TO HAVE,
IT IS NOT BASED ON WHAT WE HAVE
OR WHERE WE ARE IN LIFE.

♥▼♥▼♥▼♥▼♥▼♥▼♥▼♥▼♥▼♥▼♥▼♥▼♥▼♥

❤❤❤❤❤❤❤❤❤❤❤❤❤❤❤❤❤❤❤❤❤❤❤❤

❤ *Marinated Grilled Chicken Breast* ❤

This is delicious served with Rice-a-Roni Fried Rice with Almonds. Make as directed on Rice-a-Roni package except substitute 2 Tbs. liquid Butter Buds for margarine. Use orange slice for garnish.

1 - 16 oz. fat-free Italian dressing (I like Kraft)
4 boneless, skinless, chicken breast (all fat trimmed off)

Marinate raw chicken breast in dressing for at least 1 hour, turning over once. (Overnight is best.)

Remove chicken from salad dressing. Grill or cook in covered pan that has been sprayed with no-fat spray. Cook 5-7 minutes until there is no pink in chicken. Chicken is all white when done.

Chicken Only Yield: 4 servings   Calories: 198
                Fat: 4 grams

❤ *Southern Style Chicken Gravy &* *Biscuits* ❤

1 cup skim milk
$1/4$ cup corn starch
1 Tbs. garlic salt - optional
1 - $14^1/_2$ oz. can chicken broth (I use Campbell's)
dash of pepper - optional
3 - 8 oz. cans of no salt mixed vegetables - drained
$1^1/_2$ lbs. skinless chicken breast - fully cooked and
       shredded into bite size pieces

Put first 5 ingredients into Dutch Oven (large size) pan. Mix well before turning on heat to dissolve corn starch completely. Turn heat on medium. Add drained vegetables and cooked bite size pieces of chicken. Stir occasionally and cook for approximately 10-12 minutes until thick and creamy.

Serve $1/2$ cup over 2 biscuits (I use Four Winds Farm brand from Foodtown.) Only 100 calories and 1 gram of fat for 2 biscuits.

Yield: 10 servings (8 oz. each-biscuits not included)
             Calories: 153   Fat: 2.8 grams

❤❤❤❤❤❤❤❤❤❤❤❤❤❤❤❤❤❤❤❤❤❤❤

♥♥♥♥♥♥♥♥♥♥♥♥♥♥♥♥♥♥♥♥♥♥♥♥♥♥♥♥♥

♥ *Chicken Noodle Casserole* ♥

8 oz. fat-free shredded cheddar cheese (I use Healthy
    Choice)
4 oz. can mushrooms - drained
12 oz. bag "No Yolk" noodles
1 lb. cooked chicken breast cut into bite size pieces
3 jars Heinz Homestyle Gravy chicken flavor
1 tsp. garlic salt - optional
16 oz. mixed vegetables, drained
dash of pepper - optional
2 cups Skinny's crushed - optional (Found in low-fat
    chip aisle.)

Cook noodles as directed on package. Mix all ingredients
together with half of the cheese (use 4 oz.).

Spray a 9" x 13" pan with a non-fat cooking spray. Pour into
pan. Sprinkle remaining 4 oz. of cheese and crushed Skinny's
on top of casserole. Bake at 350 degrees for 20 minutes until
completely warmed.

Serve with grated Parmesan cheese, on the side, so that if
desired someone can sprinkle a little on.

Yield: 9 servings   Calories: 309   Fat: 2.5 grams

♥ *Beef-N-Noodles* ♥

Note: This is very good served with Potatoes A-La-Larry.

2 cups eye of round beef - cooked and shredded or 1
    lb. Healthy choice hamburger - browned
1 - 12 oz. jar of Heinz Fat-Free Seasoned Pork or Beef
    Gravy.
2 cups cooked pasta (Left over spaghetti noodles will
    work if you have them. Just soak the cooked
    spaghetti completely in a bowl of water in the
    refrigerator until you need them for this recipe.)

Mix gravy with cooked pasta and beef. Heat and serve.

Yield: 4 servings   Calories: 341   Fat: 6.2 grams

♥♥♥♥♥♥♥♥♥♥♥♥♥♥♥♥♥♥♥♥♥♥♥♥♥♥♥♥♥

❤❤❤❤❤❤❤❤❤❤❤❤❤❤❤❤❤❤❤❤❤❤❤❤❤❤❤❤

❤ *Hamburger Gravy Over Biscuits* ❤

1 lb. ground eye of round (beef)
1 packet Butter Buds - dry
3 cups skim milk
$^1/_2$ cup corn starch
2 tsp. garlic salt - optional
dash of pepper - optional

In a large pan or Dutch Oven cook on medium heat, ground
eye of round, Butter Buds, pepper and garlic salt until ground
eye of round is fully cooked. Pour 2 cups skim milk into
ground eye of round. Add corn starch to remaining 1 cup skim
milk, stirring until cornstarch is completely dissolved. Pour
into beef. Stirring constantly, cook approximately 5 minutes
longer, until thick and creamy. Serve over hot biscuits. (I use
Rightshape biscuits by Four Winds Farm, sold at Foodtown.
Only 100 calories and 1 gram of fat for two biscuits.) Pillsbury
Buttermilk Biscuits are also good.

Yield: 6 servings (w/o biscuits)   Calories: 135
                     Fat: 2.66 grams

❤ *Beef Stroganoff* ❤

*This meal is delicious with warm bread. I like to warm French bread in
the oven. People love to dip their warm French bread into the juices of the
Beef Stroganoff on their plates.*

2 lbs. partially frozen eye of round (beef)
8 oz. fresh mushrooms - sliced thin
1 large onion - sliced thin
1 tsp. garlic salt
16 oz. no-fat sour cream
$^1/_2$ cup liquid Butter Buds
12 oz. "No Yolk" brand noodles, cooked and drained
pepper to taste

Thinly slice the partially frozen beef into bite size strips,
eliminating all visible fat. Brown in large pan. Rinse beef under
water. Set aside. Combine onion, mushrooms and liquid
Butter Buds, sauté until soft. Add cooked beef, garlic salt, no-
fat sour cream, and pepper. Stir until all combined well, do
<u>NOT</u> boil.

Serve hot over warm "No Yolk" brand noodles.

Yield: 8   Calories: 361   Fat: 5.9 grams
❤❤❤❤❤❤❤❤❤❤❤❤❤❤❤❤❤❤❤❤❤❤❤❤❤❤❤❤

♥♥♥♥♥♥♥♥♥♥♥♥♥♥♥♥♥♥♥♥♥♥♥♥♥♥♥

♥ *Beefy-Chili Burritos with Cheese* ♥
My kids love to roll these up themselves.

    1 package of fat-free flour tortilla shells
    16 oz. fat-free fancy shredded cheddar cheese (I use
        Healthy Choice brand)
    1 lb. ground eye of round (beef)
    2 cans Health Valley Fat-Free Chili (15 oz. spicy
        vegetarian with black beans)

In medium pan brown ground eye of round. Add both cans of
chili and 6 oz. of cheddar cheese. Stir over medium-low heat
until cheese is completely dissolved. (About 5 minutes).

Put $1/10$ of the beefy-chili mixture in the middle of the soft taco.
Roll up. Sprinkle 1 oz. of shredded cheddar cheese on top.
Microwave about 10-15 seconds to melt cheese on top. Serve
warm.

*Garnish with your favorite salsa if desired. With a side tossed
salad and fat-free western salad dressing this is a complete,
delicious and nutritious meal!

Yield: 10 servings   Calories: 260   Fat: 4.6 grams
*Not included in calorie or fats information.

♥ *Beef Fajitas* ♥

    1 lb. cooked shredded beef or Healthy Choice ground
        beef
    $1/2$ cup fat-free Italian salad dressing
    fat-free taco or cheddar cheese
    10 soft flour taco shells (Buena Vista brand is fat free)
    1 cup shredded iceburg lettuce
    1 cup chopped tomato
    fat-free sour cream - optional

Marinate beef in dressing. Warm beef in microwave with
dressing. Microwave soft taco shell until warm.

Put desired amount of marinated beef on soft shell. Top with
lettuce, tomato, cheese and sour cream (if desired).

Without Sour Cream:
Yield: 5 servings   Calories: 420   Fat: 4.4 grams
        10 servings   Calories: 210   Fat: 2.2 grams

♥♥♥♥♥♥♥♥♥♥♥♥♥♥♥♥♥♥♥♥♥♥♥♥♥♥♥

♥♥♥♥♥♥♥♥♥♥♥♥♥♥♥♥♥♥♥♥♥♥♥♥♥♥♥♥♥♥

♥ *Dogs in a Blanket* ♥
Fast, easy and fun for kids to make.

8 Healthy Choice hot dogs
2 rolls of Rightshape biscuits (sold at Foodtown)
(You will have 4 biscuits left over)

Preheat oven to 350 degrees. Take 2 biscuits and wrap around a hot dog. Pinch biscuit dough with fingers to seal the "blanket".

Spray 2 cookie sheets with a non-fat cooking spray. Lay 4 prepared "Dogs in a Blanket" on each cookie sheet, making sure they are nicely spread apart, because the dough will get bigger as they cook.

Bake at 350 degrees for 10 minutes or until dough is golden brown.

Serve with mustard, ketchup or bar-b-que sauce on the side for dipping.

Yield: 8 servings   Calories: 150   Fat: 2 grams

♥ *Cheesie Dogs in a Blanket* ♥

4 slices fat-free cheese

Follow above recipe exactly, except cut hot dogs ¹/₂ way through lengthwise to make just enough room for ¹/₂ slice of fat-free cheese to slip in. Wrap with dough. Bake exactly as above.

Yield: 8 servings   Calories: 170   Fat: 2 grams

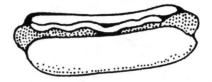

HOW CAN WE HOPE FOR GREATER GIFTS
AND TALENTS FROM GOD
IF WE DON'T EVEN USE THE ONES WE'VE GOT?

♥♥♥♥♥♥♥♥♥♥♥♥♥♥♥♥♥♥♥♥♥♥♥♥♥♥♥♥♥♥

♥♥♥♥♥♥♥♥♥♥♥♥♥♥♥♥♥♥♥♥♥♥♥♥♥♥♥♥♥

❤ *Dogs on a Stick* ❤

Fast, easy and fun for kids to make.

corn meal - optional
8 Oscar Mayer fat-free hot dogs
2 rolls of Rightshape biscuits (you'll have 4 biscuits left over)
8 popsicle sticks

Preheat oven to 350 degrees.

Take 2 biscuits and wrap around hot dog, pinching biscuit dough with fingers to seal the dough around the hot dogs.

Place 1 popsicle stick ¹/₂ way through the hot dog, leaving ¹/₂ of the stick sticking out to later use as a stick.

Arrange "dogs on a stick" on 2 cookie sheets that have been sprayed with a non-fat cooking spray, making sure they are nicely separated because the dough will get bigger as they cook and you don't want them to stick to each other. Sprinkle with corn meal if desired, before baking.

Bake at 350 degrees for 10 minutes or until dough is golden brown. Serve with mustard or ketchup.

Yield: 8 servings   Calories: 153   Fat: 2 grams

❤ *Pigs on a Stick* ❤

Substitute Healthy Choice smoked sausage for the hot dogs.

Cut sausage into 8 pieces. Wrap each sausage with 2 biscuits (you'll have 4 biscuits left over). Follow directions above as in "Dogs on a Stick".

Yield: 8 servings   Calories: 161   Fat: 4.1 grams

PRAY EVERY DAY AND HOPE FOR THE BEST.

♥♥♥♥♥♥♥♥♥♥♥♥♥♥♥♥♥♥♥♥♥♥♥♥♥♥♥♥♥

♥ *Pigs in a Blanket* ♥

Fast, easy and fun for kids to make.

14 oz. Healthy Choice smoked sausage
2 rolls of Rightshape biscuits - you'll have 4 biscuits
    left over

Preheat oven to 350 degrees.

Cut smoked sausage into 8 pieces. It will look like short, fat
little hot dogs. Wrap each little sausage with two biscuits.
Pinch biscuit dough with fingers to seal the "Blanket". Spray 2
cookie sheets with a non-fat spray.

Bake at 350 degrees for 10 minutes or until dough is golden
brown. Serve with mustard, ketchup or bar-b-que sauce for
dipping.

Yield: 8 servings   Calories: 161   Fat: 4.1 grams

♥ *Sausage Skillet Dinner* ♥

A complete meal in itself that is fast, easy and delicious.

2 - 15¹/₂ oz. French style green beans with its juices
1 medium onion - chopped
1 - 14-16 oz. Healthy Choice smoked sausage - cut into
    bite size pieces
1 packet Butter Buds - dry
1 tsp. garlic salt - optional
dash of pepper - optional
4 medium potatoes

Cut sausage into bite size pieces. Spray a non-fat cooking
spray on bottom of large skillet. Brown sausage. In the
meantime cook potatoes in microwave until done.
(Approximately 5 - 10 minutes. Potatoes will be firm yet soft
when done.)

Add chopped onions, Butter Buds, garlic salt and pepper.
Cover and sauté for 5 minutes, with the meat and green
beans.

By this time the potatoes are done. Cut potatoes into bite size
pieces. Toss with the rest of the food in the skillet. Cover and
let simmer about 5 more minutes.

Yield: 6 servings   Calories: 180   Fat: 0.9 grams

♥♥♥♥♥♥♥♥♥♥♥♥♥♥♥♥♥♥♥♥♥♥♥♥♥♥

♥ *Pizza Pasta* ♥

2 - 7¼ oz. boxes of macaroni and cheese mix
1 envelope Butter Buds - dry
1 cup skim milk
1 - 14 oz. jar Prego Pizza Sauce with Ground Sausage
8 oz. fat-free shredded cheese (if desired)

Prepare macaroni as directed on box, substituting dry Butter Buds for butter and 1 cup skim milk instead of ½ cup milk.

Once cheese is well mixed in, add pizza sauce. Mix well.

Top with fat-free cheese if desired. Broil in oven at 425 degrees for 3 minutes or until cheese is melted.

Serve hot.

This can be made in advance, frozen and baked at 350 degrees for 35-45 minutes when needed.

Yield: 8 servings   Calories: 203   Fat: 2.5 grams

BEING A MODEST GOOD WINNER IS JUST AS IMPORTANT AS NOT BEING A POOR LOSER.

♥♥♥♥♥♥♥♥♥♥♥♥♥♥♥♥♥♥♥♥♥♥♥♥♥♥

❤ *Asparagus Casserole Dinner* ❤

8 redskin potatoes
$^1/_2$ lb. turkey ham (or very lean ham) - chopped thinly
1 lb. fresh mushrooms - thinly sliced
1 packet Butter Buds - dry
8 oz. fat-free Healthy Choice Cheddar Cheese
2 - 15 oz. cans long stem asparagus

In skillet sprayed with a non-fat cooking spray, sauté mushrooms and ham together along with the dry packet of Butter Buds.

In the meantime microwave the redskin potatoes until cooked. (It only takes a few minutes. Potatoes are tender when done.)

Cut cooked redskins into $^1/_3$" slices. Arrange sliced cooked redskins on a 9" x 13" pan that has been sprayed with a non-fat cooking spray. Spread sauteed mushrooms and ham over potatoes. Arrange asparagus spears in strips. Sprinkle cheddar cheese over asparagus, ham and mushrooms.

Broil for 3-5 minutes or until top of cheese is golden brown and hot.

Yield: 6 servings   Calories: 256   Fat: 1.5 grams

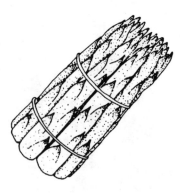

COMMIT YOURSELF TO GOD, YOUR MARRIAGE, YOUR
HEALTH AND YOUR FAMILY EVERYDAY.

♥♥♥♥♥♥♥♥♥♥♥♥♥♥♥♥♥♥♥♥♥♥♥♥

♥ *Sauerkraut Spaghetti* ♥

I know this recipe sounds crazy. To be honest, when I heard it from a friend I thought she was nuts, but my curiosity killed the cat! It's really good!

For however much you want to make, use this formula. This is for one serving.

> $^1/_2$ cup sauerkraut
> $^3/_4$ cup of your favorite spaghetti sauce (mine is Prego Extra Chunky Garden Combination)

Drain sauerkraut and rinse. Squeeze dry. Mix spaghetti sauce with sauerkraut. Warm in the microwave. Sprinkle with grated parmesan cheese if desired. Serve warm.

Serving Size: 1$^1/_4$ cup serving size   Calories: 170
                              Fat: 2 grams
Calories can be cut 40% by using Healthy Choice Spaghetti Sauce.

♥ *Mexican Spaghetti* ♥

For fast & easy Mexican Spaghetti Salad do the exact same thing but serve chilled.

2 cups *shredded cooked beef
2 cups cooked spaghetti
1 - 16 oz. jar of your favorite salsa
finely grated fat-free taco or cheddar cheese - optional

Toss 1st three ingredients together. Top with cheese if desired. Microwave until warm. Serve warm.

Serve extra warmed up salsa on the side if desired.

*Use leftover eye of round roast

Yield: 4 servings   Calories: 260   Fat: 5.8 grams

♥♥♥♥♥♥♥♥♥♥♥♥♥♥♥♥♥♥♥♥♥♥♥♥

♥♥♥♥♥♥♥♥♥♥♥♥♥♥♥♥♥♥♥♥♥♥♥♥♥♥♥

Fast & Easy Original Magic Pockets

These tasty delectables are fun for children to help make. Once I created one, it put me on a roll and I've created many different flavors. Don't limit yourself to just the ones I've created. Create some of your own!

♥ Ham & Cheese Magic Pockets ♥

³/₄ lb. turkey ham - chopped into ¹/₄" pieces
1 cup fat-free cheddar cheese (I used Healthy Choice)
¹/₂ cup mushrooms - chopped (optional)
2 Tbs. fat-free honey dijon salad dressing
3 cans of low-fat biscuit dough - 10 in each can (I used
     Four Winds brand, 100 cal. and 1 gram of fat for 2)
2 egg whites

Beat egg whites - set aside. Spray 2 cookie sheets with a non-fat cooking spray. With hands flatten each biscuit into a thin, flat piece of round dough. (That's where I have my children help out. While I'm chopping the ingredients, they flatten out the dough.)

Arrange 15 individual flattened dough pieces on 2 cookie sheets making sure they do not touch. Lay extra dough pieces on wax paper until ready to use. Brush each dough piece with egg whites. (The beaten egg whites are the glue which holds the crust together and seals it shut.) Set aside.

In a bowl combine chopped ham, cheese, mushrooms and honey dijon salad dressing. Mix until well coated with dressing. Put a good size rounded tablespoon of meat and cheese concoction in the center of each flattened dough piece on cookie sheet. Using remaining flattened dough previously set aside, with hands cover each one, one at a time. Brush sides with egg whites. Using a fork seal dough edges. Brush top with egg whites.

Bake at 375 degrees for 15 minutes.

Yield: 15 servings   Calories: 152   Fat: 1.4 grams

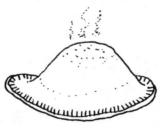

♥♥♥♥♥♥♥♥♥♥♥♥♥♥♥♥♥♥♥♥♥♥♥♥♥♥♥

♥♥♥♥♥♥♥♥♥♥♥♥♥♥♥♥♥♥♥♥♥♥♥♥♥♥♥♥♥

♥ *South of the Border Magic Pockets* ♥

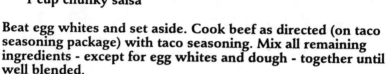

6 cans of low-fat biscuit dough
1 lb. ground eye of round
1 envelope taco seasoning for meat
1 cup corn
2 cups fat-free shredded cheddar cheese
2 tbs. sugar
1 cup chunky salsa

Beat egg whites and set aside. Cook beef as directed (on taco seasoning package) with taco seasoning. Mix all remaining ingredients - except for egg whites and dough - together until well blended.

Spray 4 cookie sheets with a non-fat cooking spray. With hands flatten 30 of the biscuits into round flat pieces on the cookie sheet. Make sure the edges do not touch each other. Brush each flattened dough piece with egg whites on the edges of the dough. Put one rounded tablespoon of meat concoction into center of each piece of flattened dough. With hands flatten one remaining biscuit for each pocket and cover each pocket one at a time. Seal dough edges together with fork.

Brush tops of each pocket with beaten egg whites. Sprinkle with paprika if desired.

Bake at 375 degrees for 15 minutes.

Yield: 30 pockets   Calories: 171   Fat: 2.3 grams

♥ *South of the Border Hot Dogs* ♥

A Mexican twist to an all American food.

1 pkg. Oscar Mayer Fat-Free Hot dogs (8 count)
1 pkg. Aunt Millies Fat-Free Hot dog Buns
8 Tbs. chunky salsa - your favorite brand
8 Tbs. grated fat-free cheddar cheese

Put 1 hot dog in each bun. Top with 1 Tbs. grated cheddar cheese and 1 Tbs. salsa. Microwave each on high for approximately 45 seconds to 1 minute. Enjoy!!

Yield: 8 servings   Calories: 185   Fat: 0 grams

♥♥♥♥♥♥♥♥♥♥♥♥♥♥♥♥♥♥♥♥♥♥♥♥♥♥♥

♥ *Pizza Magic Pockets* ♥

1 cup fat-free mozzarella finely shredded cheese (I use
    Healthy Choice)
¹/₂ cup mushroom or green pepper (Use any
    combination you desire)
1 lb. ground eye of round
¹/₂ cup of your favorite pizza sauce (I like Prego)
2 egg whites
3 cans of low-fat biscuit dough - 10 in each can. (I use
    Four Winds brand)
garlic salt - optional

Brown beef. Drain fat if needed. Set aside.

Beat egg whites - set aside.

Spray 2 cookie sheets with a non-fat cooking spray.

With hands flatten each biscuit into a thin, flat piece of round
dough. Arrange 15 individual flattened dough pieces on 2
cookie sheets, making sure they do not touch. Brush each
dough piece with beaten egg whites. Set aside.

In a bowl mix cheese, mushroom, green pepper, browned eye
of round and pizza sauce together until well coated with
sauce. Put a good size rounded tablespoon of meat and cheese
concoction in the center of each flattened dough piece on
cookie sheet. Using remaining flattened dough pieces
previously set aside, with hands cover each one one at a time.
Brush sides with egg whites. Using a fork, seal dough edges.
Brush top with egg whites. Lightly sprinkle tops with garlic
salt. (If desired.)

Bake at 375 degrees for 15 minutes.

Yield: 15 servings   Calories: 164   Fat: 2.4 grams

THE PRETTIEST THING YOU CAN WEAR IS A SMILE.

♥♥♥♥♥♥♥♥♥♥♥♥♥♥♥♥♥♥♥♥♥♥♥♥♥♥♥

♥ *Steak & Onion Philly Magic Pockets* ♥

3 cans of low-fat biscuit dough
$^3/_4$ lb. eye of round beef - sliced into very thin strips,
    $^1/_4$" or $^1/_2$" long
1 cup fat-free shredded mozzarella cheese (I use
    Healthy Choice)
2 egg whites
$^1/_4$ cup of your favorite steak sauce (I like Heinz 57
    sauce)
$^1/_2$ cup onion - finely chopped

Beat egg whites and set aside. Spray 2 cookie sheets with a
non-fat cooking spray.

With hands flatten each biscuit into a thin flat piece of round
dough. Saute onions with beef over low heat until thoroughly
cooked (4-7 minutes). Remove from heat and let cool. Add
steak sauce and cheese. Mix until well blended.

Arrange 15 pieces of flattened round dough pieces on cookie
sheets so that sides do not touch. Brush sides with beaten egg
whites. Put a good size tablespoon of meat and cheese
concoction in the center of each flattened dough piece on
cookie sheet. Using remaining flattened dough pieces,
previously set aside, with hands cover each one, one at a time.

With fork seal dough edges together. Brush top with egg
whites.

Bake at 375 degrees for 15 minutes.

Yield: 15 servings   Calories: 156   Fat: 2.1 grams

♥ *Chili Mac* ♥

Great with corn bread.

2 - 15 oz. cans Health Valley Fat-Free Spicy Vegetarian
    Chili with Black Beans
1 lb. macaroni (I like to use shell shaped)
1 lb. ground eye of round (beef)

Cook macaroni as directed on box. Brown eye of round. Stir
together chili, eye of round and macaroni. Serve warm!

Yield: 10 servings   Calories: 257   Fat: 2.9 grams

♥♥♥♥♥♥♥♥♥♥♥♥♥♥♥♥♥♥♥♥♥♥♥♥♥♥

♥♥♥♥♥♥♥♥♥♥♥♥♥♥♥♥♥♥♥♥♥♥♥♥♥♥♥♥♥

♥ Open Faced Fresh Tomato Sandwiches ♥

Kids Cookin'

2 Father Sam's pocket bread - mini size
8 tsp. Seven Seas fat-free ranch salad dressing
1 med. fresh tomato - try to find the deepest red colored one

Cut pockets in half. Toast each half. Spread 2 tsp. salad
dressing on each half. Cut tomato into 4 slices. Put one slice
tomato on each half of toasted pocket bread that has been
spread with salad dressing.

Eat immediately.

Yield: 4 servings   Calorie: 72   Fat: 0 grams

♥ Complete Turkey & Dressing Dinner ♥

*This is so easy, that it's almost embarrassing. But don't worry - I'm not!
This recipe can be made days in advance and refrigerated until ready to
bake. Just cook a little longer to make sure it's completely warmed.*

1 box Stove Top stuffing - chicken or turkey flavor (6
    serving size)
2 cups hot water
12 oz. turkey breast lunchmeat (I use Mr. Turkey brand)
1 - 15 oz. can green beans - drained
2 envelopes of Butter Buds
1 jar of Heinz Homestyle Roasted Turkey Gravy (12 oz.
    size)
pepper to season - optional

In medium size bowl, mix seasoning from stuffing box with
bread crumbs, water and one envelope Butter Buds. Set aside.

Spray a 9" x 13" pan with a non-fat cooking spray. Spread
prepared stuffing mixture evenly on bottom of pan. Arrange
turkey lunchmeat slices on top of stuffing. (Edges of
lunchmeat will overlap.) Spread gravy evenly over turkey
Drain juices from green beans. Evenly arrange green beans on
top of gravy. Sprinkle green beans with one envelope of Butter
Buds. (And pepper if desired). Cover pan with foil and bake
covered at 350 degrees for 30-35 minutes, until completely
warmed.

Yield: 6 servings   Calories: 225   Fat: 5 grams

♥♥♥♥♥♥♥♥♥♥♥♥♥♥♥♥♥♥♥♥♥♥♥♥♥♥♥♥♥

♥♥♥♥♥♥♥♥♥♥♥♥♥♥♥♥♥♥♥♥♥♥♥♥♥♥♥♥

♥ *Cherry Breakfast Sandwich* ♥

*A meal in itself! Looks like a sandwich,
but eat it with a fork.*

2 Special K Fat-Free Waffles
¹/₂ cup lite cherry pie filling (warm in the microwave if
    desired)
1 Tbs. blueberry lite syrup

Toast waffles until golden brown. Spread cherry pie filling on
top of one waffle. Put second waffle on top of cherries. Drizzle
syrup over top of second waffle, allowing syrup to run over
the edges. Serve immediately.

Yield: 1 serving   Calories: 219   Fat: 0 grams

♥ *Breakfast Sandwich* ♥

1 Aunt Millies Lite Fat-Free Potato Hamburger Bun
2 egg whites
pepper to taste (if desired)
3 slices thin sliced ham (I use Hillshire Farm Deli Select -
    10 calories per slice)
1 slice fat-free cheddar cheese (I use Kraft Free)

Spray griddle with no-fat cooking spray. Spray biscuit cutter
inside with no-fat cooking spray. Beat egg whites. Put sprayed
biscuit cutter onto sprayed griddle. Pour eggs into middle of
biscuit cutter. In the meantime spray insides of hamburger
buns with no-fat cooking spray and brown (toast) the buns on
griddle. Warm ham slices on griddle. Cut cheese slice in half
and lay on top of ham slices being warmed on the griddle.
Once everything is cooked lay ham slices with cheese on
bottom part of the browned hamburger bun. Lay cooked egg
on top of ham and cheese. Put top of hamburger bun on and
presto! Breakfast!! (Some people like mustard on this
sandwich.)

Yield: 1 serving   Calories: 190   Fat: 1 gram

A HAPPY HEART IS A THANKFUL HEART.

♥♥♥♥♥♥♥♥♥♥♥♥♥♥♥♥♥♥♥♥♥♥♥♥♥♥♥♥

♥♥♥♥♥♥♥♥♥♥♥♥♥♥♥♥♥♥♥♥♥♥♥♥♥♥♥

♥ *Baked French Toast* ♥

What's great about this recipe is it can be prepared in advance and kept in the fridge (if desired) before baking.

12 slices of raisin bread
1 cup skim milk
8 egg whites
$^1/_4$ cup packed brown sugar
1 tsp. vanilla

Spray a jellyroll pan (a cookie sheet with $^1/_2$" sides) with a non-fat cooking spray. Lay 12 slices of raisin bread in 3 rows of 4, sides of bread will be touching. If bread is slightly stale or dry that's fine.

Beat milk, egg whites, brown sugar and vanilla on high with mixer for $1^1/_2$ - 2 minutes. Pour mixture over slices of bread. Once bread is all wet turn each slice over to guarantee all bread is wet.

Bake at 325 degrees for 27-30 minutes. Serve immediately. Sprinkle powdered sugar lightly on top or syrup if desired.

Yield: 6 - 2 slice servings   Calories: 200
Fat: 2 grams

YOUR HOME SHOULD BE YOUR HAVEN OF REST.

♥♥♥♥♥♥♥♥♥♥♥♥♥♥♥♥♥♥♥♥♥♥♥♥♥♥♥

Desserts

Mini Contents

(Desserts)

I'VE LEARNED TO BITE MY TONGUE (VERSUS GIVING MY
OPINION WHEN NOT ASKED). IT'S TO THE POINT THAT
I'VE ALMOST BITTEN A HOLE THROUGH IT!

❤❤❤❤❤❤❤❤❤❤❤❤❤❤❤❤❤❤❤❤❤❤❤❤❤

❤ *Warm Fruit Cocktail Dessert* ❤
Great for cold, snowy days.

Kids Cookin'

1 - 16 oz. lite fruit cocktail
1 - 9 oz. Jiffy Golden Yellow Cake mix
Lite Cool Whip

Drain juice from fruit cocktail. Beat cake mix and fruit cocktail juice until well blended. Pour fruit into cake batter. Gently mix fruit into cake batter until well blended with spoon.

Spray 8" x 8" or a 9" x 9" square cake pan with a non-fat cooking spray. Pour cake batter into prepared pan.

Bake at 350 degrees for 40-45 minutes or until top is golden brown. Serve warm with Lite Cool Whip. You need to spoon out this dessert; it will not cut.

Yield: 9 servings
Fat: 2 grams

Calories: 133
(not including Lite Cool Whip)

❤ *City Slicker S'more Balls* ❤
*Fun for kids to make! A neat indoor twist to S'mores
that we make when we are camping.*

2 Tbs. Fat-Free Ultra Promise Margarine
2 cups mini-marshmallows
60 chocolate chips
3 cups Golden Grahams Cereal

Over low heat melt Fat-Free Promise with mini-marshmallows, stirring constantly.

When marshmallows have melted down to $\frac{1}{2}$ of their original size remove from heat. Add cereal and mix well. (Don't let marshmallows melt completely).

Spray hands with a non-fat cooking spray. Divide mixture into 15 parts. Roll each part with hands and form into balls. Place 4 chocolate chips throughout each ball.

Set each ball on wax paper and let cool completely.

Yield: 15 servings
Calories: 55
Fat: .73 grams

❤❤❤❤❤❤❤❤❤❤❤❤❤❤❤❤❤❤❤❤❤❤❤❤❤

❤ *Sweet & Heavenly Twinkie Dessert* ❤

2¹/₂ cups fresh strawberries - cleaned & cut into bite size
    pieces
1 cup sugar
3 Tbs. cornstarch
2 Tbs. Lite Karo Syrup
1 cup water
1 box sugar-free strawberry Jello - dry
9 Hostess Light Twinkies - cut in ¹/₂ lengthwise
¹/₄ cup Lite Cool Whip

In saucepan over medium-low heat bring to a boil the sugar,
cornstarch, syrup and water. Stirring occasionally, cook until it
becomes clear in color.

Remove from heat. Let cool a couple of minutes.

In the meantime, cut the "Twinkies" in ¹/₂ lengthwise. Place
with cream side up. Line a 9" x 13" pan with the cut
"Twinkies". Edges will be touching.

Stir strawberry sugar-free Jello into clear mixture which has
cooled slightly. Mix well until it is one smooth color of red.
Add strawberries.

Spread strawberries over "Twinkies." Refrigerate for 5
minutes before serving.

Top with a dab of Lite Cool Whip and drizzle it throughout
the top of the dessert with knife to make it look pretty.

Yield: 15 servings   Calories: 138
                                   Fat: 1.06 grams

BE A "GOD PLEASER", NOT A MAN PLEASER.

♥♥♥♥♥♥♥♥♥♥♥♥♥♥♥♥♥♥♥♥♥♥♥♥♥♥♥♥♥

♥ *Cherry Berry Dessert Waffles* ♥

*This is a beautiful dessert to the eyes and a special dessert for any
occasion. This is so filling that I eat it as a meal.*

1 Special K Fat-Free Waffle
¹/₂ cup lite cherry pie filling (Meijer has a good inexpensive
     brand)
3 oz. sugar-free, fat-free blueberry ribbon dessert (I use
     Superior Dairy Brand)
1 Tbs. Lite Cool Whip
1 Tbs. blueberry lite syrup (I like to use Featherweight
     brand)

Pop one waffle into the toaster until golden brown. While still
warm put blueberry ribbon frozen dessert on waffle. Top
with lite cherry pie filling and add a dab of Lite Cool Whip on
top of cherry pie filling. Drizzle lite blueberry syrup over Cool
Whip and cherries.

Serve immediately.

Yield: 1 serving   Calories: 248 Fat: 0 grams

♥ *Whitney Crispies* ♥

An excellent twist to an old favorite!
(Created by my 6 year old daughter Whitney)

1 tsp. peanut butter flavor extract
¹/₄ cup Fat-Free Ultra Promise Margarine
10 oz. package mini-marshmallows + 1 cup mini-
     marshmallows
5 cups toasted rice cereal
¹/₃ cup fat-free chocolate frosting (recipe in book) or use
     Lovin' Lites Chocolate Frosting already prepared

Spray Dutch Oven (large saucepan) with a non-fat cooking
spray. Melt together margarine, marshmallows and peanut
butter extract. Remove from heat. Stir in cereal. Press into a 9"
x 13" pan that has been sprayed with a non-fat cooking spray.

Let cool. Frost with lite chocolate frosting.

Yield: 15 servings   Calories: 124
Fat: 0 grams

♥♥♥♥♥♥♥♥♥♥♥♥♥♥♥♥♥♥♥♥♥♥♥♥♥♥♥♥♥

♥♥♥♥♥♥♥♥♥♥♥♥♥♥♥♥♥♥♥♥♥♥♥♥♥♥♥♥

 ♥ *Chocolate Mousse* ♥

1 box sugar-free instant chocolate pudding mix (4 serving size)
3 Tbs. fat-free hot fudge syrup (I use Smuckers)
1 8 oz. Lite Cool Whip

Mix all together until smooth.

Serve chilled.

Yield: 6 servings　　　Calories: 99　　　Fat: 2.5 grams

 ♥ *Chocolate Cherry Mousse* ♥

1 large sugar free chocolate pudding mix (6 serving)
1 pkg. Dream Whip
1$^{1}/_{2}$ cups cold skim milk
1 - 15 oz. can lite cherry pie filling - chilled

Mix (everything except cherries) well and blend until thick, about 3 minutes. Starting with and ending with cherry pie filling, alternate chocolate mousse and pie filling in a pretty glass. (Wine glasses, dessert cups, etc.) Keep chilled in refrigerator until ready to serve.

Yield: 10 servings　　　Fat: 1 gram

♥ *Warm Baked Peach Dessert* ♥

1 - 29 oz. can peaches in light syrup or own juices
$^{1}/_{4}$ cup Mrs. Richardson Butterscotch Caramel Fudge Topping
1 - 7 oz. box Health Valley Fat-Free Peach Apricot Mini Fruit Center Cookie

Pour peaches with juices in a 8" x 10" pan. Crumble cookies on top. Microwave caramel fudge on high for 10-15 seconds. (Just enough to drizzle.) Drizzle caramel over cookie crumbs. Bake at 350 degrees for 20 minutes. Serve hot from the oven.

Great with fat-free frozen vanilla yogurt.

Yield: 6 servings　　　Calories: 169　　　Fat: 0.1 grams

TAKE TIME TO BE LOVING EVERYDAY.

♥♥♥♥♥♥♥♥♥♥♥♥♥♥♥♥♥♥♥♥♥♥♥♥♥♥♥♥

♥♥♥♥♥♥♥♥♥♥♥♥♥♥♥♥♥♥♥♥♥♥♥♥♥♥♥♥

♥ *Cinnamon Krispie Squares* ♥

If you like Rice Krispie Squares and you like cinnamon you'll love these.

> 10.5 oz. bag mini marshmallows
> 8 cups Apple Cinnamon Rice Krispies (Kellogg's brand)
> 3 Tbs. Ultra Fat-Free Promise Margarine
> 2 tsp. cinnamon
> 1 tsp. Nutra-Sweet® Spoonful™ (OR 1 tsp. sugar)

Spray a 9" x 13" pan with non-fat cooking spray. Set aside.

Mix 1 tsp. cinnamon and 1 tsp. Nutra-Sweet together. Set aside.

In large Dutch Oven pan over low heat melt Fat-Free Promise and marshmallows together with 1 tsp. cinnamon, stirring constantly. Once marshmallows are melted, remove from heat. Stir in the Apple Cinnamon Rice Krispies. Mix until well coated with marshmallow mixture.

Press into prepared 9" x 13" pan. Sprinkle top with prepared cinnamon/Nutra-Sweet topping.

Refrigerate for 15 minutes. Cut into 30 squares.

Yield: 30 servings
   With Nutra-Sweet® Spoonful™: Calories: 76   Fat: 0 grams
   With sugar: Calories: 77   Fat: 0 grams

IF YOU ARE NOT CHARITABLE WITH WHAT LITTLE
WEALTH YOU HAVE NOW,
HOW CAN YOU THINK YOU'D BE MORE CHARITABLE IF
YOU HAD EVEN MORE WEALTH?

♥♥♥♥♥♥♥♥♥♥♥♥♥♥♥♥♥♥♥♥♥♥♥♥♥♥♥♥

♥♥♥♥♥♥♥♥♥♥♥♥♥♥♥♥♥♥♥♥♥♥♥♥♥♥♥

Kids Cookin' ♥ *Fat-Free Granola Bars* ♥

*This homemade version will save you bundles of money!

10.5 oz. bag of miniature marshmallows
1/4 cup Ultra Fat-Free Promise Margarine
2 cups Rice Krispies
3 1/2 cups fat-free granola (I use Health Valley brand - 12 oz.)
1/2 cup raisins

In a large Dutch Oven pan melt Ultra Fat-Free Promise with marshmallows over low heat, stirring constantly. Once marshmallows are melted, remove from heat. Add granola, raisins and Rice Krispies. Mix well.

Spray a cookie sheet with edges (approximately 15" x 10" with 1/2" edge) with a non-fat cooking spray. Pour onto sheet. Spray palm of hand with no-fat spray. With palm of hand press granola mixture firmly down. Let cool.

Cut into 20 bars. Wrap individual bars with plastic wrap. Keep in a cool, dry place.

* For tropical fat-free granola bars: Substitute 1/4 cup chopped dried pineapple and 1/4 cup chopped dried papaya for the raisins.

* For berry granola bars: Substitute 1/2 cup dried cranberries.

Yield: 20 bars   Calories: 126   Fat: 0 grams

Kids Cookin' ♥ *Blueberry Drops* ♥

2 cups blueberry pie filling (21 oz. can minus 2 tablespoons)
2 angel food cake mixes (16 oz. size) (I use Pillsbury)

Mix pie filling with cake mixes. (You may want to start with the pie filling and slowly add 1 cup of the cake mix at a time as the cake mix is super light).

Drop by teaspoons onto cookie sheet sprayed with non-fat cooking spray. Bake 8-10 minutes - until bottoms are golden brown. Once cooled the golden brown bottoms will be crispy.

Yield: 8 dozen   Calories: 42 per cookie   Fat: .009 grams

♥♥♥♥♥♥♥♥♥♥♥♥♥♥♥♥♥♥♥♥♥♥♥♥♥♥♥

♥♥♥♥♥♥♥♥♥♥♥♥♥♥♥♥♥♥♥♥♥♥♥♥♥♥♥♥

♥ *Butterscotch Cake Sundaes* ♥

1 - 12 oz. angel food cake (or use 12 oz. of larger cake if
    needed)
1 oz. finely chopped pecans
4 serving size fat-free butterscotch pudding mix - prepare
    as directed on box. (Or you could substitute an already
    prepared fat-free pudding, in the dairy section)
8 tsp. fat-free hot fudge - warmed

Prepare pudding as directed on box. After it has thickened,
tear the angel food cake up into bite size pieces and put into
the pudding. Add half of the finely chopped pecans to
pudding. Mix pudding, cake and pecans by hand until cake
pieces are well coated with pudding. At this time you can
either put it into 8 individual dessert cups or into a large
serving bowl.

If using 8 individual dessert cups: spoon into cups equally.
Microwave hot fudge until easy to drizzle. Drizzle 1 teaspoon
hot fudge over each individual dessert. Sprinkle a little
chopped pecans on each dessert. Keep refrigerated until ready
to serve. Serve chilled.

If using one large serving bowl: Microwave hot fudge until
easy to drizzle. Drizzle 8 teaspoons over dessert. Sprinkle
remaining chopped pecans over hot fudge. Keep refrigerated
until ready to serve. Serve chilled.

Yield: 8 servings   Calories: 175
                       Fat: 2.5 grams

**IF YOU THINK YOU'VE LEARNED ALL THERE IS TO
KNOW THEN YOU'RE DUMBER THAN YOU THINK!**

ALWAYS KEEP LEARNING AND KEEP TRYING.

♥♥♥♥♥♥♥♥♥♥♥♥♥♥♥♥♥♥♥♥♥♥♥♥♥♥♥♥

♥♥♥♥♥♥♥♥♥♥♥♥♥♥♥♥♥♥♥♥♥♥♥♥♥♥♥♥

♥ *Chocolate Cheesecake* ♥

¹/₂ cup Ultra Promise - melted
2 packets Equal® (OR 1 tbs. and 1 tsp. sugar)
graham cracker crumbs from mix

Mix together well. Press with fork into a 9" x 13" pan that's
been sprayed with a non-fat cooking spray.

2 pkgs. lite Royal brand cheesecake (9 oz. size)
1 pkg. sugar-free instant chocolate pudding
2 Tbs. cocoa (baking cocoa)
6 packets of Equal® (OR ¹/₄ c. sugar)
3 cups skim milk

Beat above ingredients 3 minutes on low.

Pour cream mixture over crust.

Melt ¹/₃ jar Smuckers fat-free hot fudge in microwave. With
spoon drizzle hot fudge over chocolate cheesecake.

Refrigerate. Serve chilled.

Yield: 20 servings   With Equal®: Calories: 125   Fat: 2.5 grams
                      With sugar: Calories: 137   Fat: 2.5 grams

**THOSE WHO ARE THANKFUL FOR THE LITTLE THINGS IN
LIFE ARE THE ONES WHO ENJOY LIFE TO THE FULLEST.**

♥♥♥♥♥♥♥♥♥♥♥♥♥♥♥♥♥♥♥♥♥♥♥♥♥♥♥♥

❤❤❤❤❤❤❤❤❤❤❤❤❤❤❤❤❤❤❤❤❤❤❤❤❤

❤ *Flower Pot Pudding* ❤ *Kids Cookin'*

Set a gummy worm next to flowers for fun if you'd like.

1 - sugar-free chocolate pudding (4 serving size)
8 reduced fat Snackwell's chocolate cream filled cookies -
   with creme removed
4 small flower pots or foam coffee cups
4 small bouquet of flowers - silk
4 gummy worms - optional

Crush cookies, set aside. Prepare pudding as directed on box
(with skim milk). Put ⅛ of cookie crumbs in bottom of each
flower pot or coffee cup. Put ¼ of pudding in each cup. Top
each with remaining cookie crumbs. Stick small bouquet in
each pot. Chill.

Serve chilled.

Yield: 4 servings   Calories: 132   Fat: 2.8 grams

❤ *Super Good Cherry Pineapple Cake* ❤

So Good! So Delicious! So Easy! *Kids Cookin'*

1 Lovin' Lites white cake mix
1 - 21 oz. cherry pie filling - lite
1 - 20 oz. can crushed pineapple

Drain juice from pineapple. Mix above ingredients all together.
Spread in a 9" x 13" cake pan that has been sprayed with a
non-fat cooking spray and floured.

Bake 30-35 minutes at 350 degrees. (Until knife inserted in
center comes out clean.)

Is excellent served warm with Dream Whip or no-fat frozen
yogurt.

Yield: 15 servings.   Calories: 163
                             Fat: 2.0 grams

HANG AROUND QUALITY PEOPLE.

❤❤❤❤❤❤❤❤❤❤❤❤❤❤❤❤❤❤❤❤❤❤❤❤❤

♥♥♥♥♥♥♥♥♥♥♥♥♥♥♥♥♥♥♥♥♥♥♥♥♥♥♥♥♥♥

♥ Tootie-Fruity Coffee Cake ♥

Use as a coffee cake for breakfast or use as a snack cake.

1 box of Lovin' Lites Yellow Cake Mix
2 egg whites
1 - 16 oz. can lite fruit cocktail

Beat eggs until bubbly. Add fruit cocktail with its juices and
cake mix. At low speed beat until well blended. Spread into 9"
x 13" pan that has been sprayed with a non-fat cooking spray.

Topping:
  1 envelope of Dream Whip - dry
  2 Tbs. powdered sugar
  1 tsp. cinnamon
  ⅓ cup flour

Mix topping ingredients by hand until well blended. Sprinkle
on top of cake. Bake cake with topping at 350 degrees for 30
minutes. Knife inserted in middle will come out clean.

Yield: 15 servings   Calories: 173
                             Fat: 2.5 grams

♥ Whatcha'Macallit Sundae ♥

This is so rich you may want to share.

1 - 1.1 oz. fat-free brownie
½ cup fat-free chocolate frozen yogurt
1 Tbs. Hershey Fat-Free Syrup
1 Tbs. Mrs. Richardson's Fat-Free Butterscotch Caramel
    Fudge Syrup
11 chocolate chips
3 Snackwell's Mini Chocolate Chip cookies

Top the fat-free brownie with fat-free chocolate frozen yogurt,
Hershey's Syrup, butterscotch caramel fudge, chocolate chips
and finish off with 3 Snackwell's Mini-Chocolate Chip Cookies
- broken up.

Serve immediately.

(Triple this recipe, add pickle spears and serve at 3 a.m. It'll
satisfy any pregnant lady's late night cravings!)

1 serving: Calories: 385   Fat: 1.5 grams
2 servings: Calories: 192   Fat: .75 grams
♥♥♥♥♥♥♥♥♥♥♥♥♥♥♥♥♥♥♥♥♥♥♥♥♥♥♥♥♥♥

♥♥♥♥♥♥♥♥♥♥♥♥♥♥♥♥♥♥♥♥♥♥♥♥♥♥

♥ *Apple Cinnamon Cake* ♥

1 box yellow light cake mix (I use Betty Crocker Super
    Moist brand)
1¹/₂ cup unsweetened applesauce
2 tsp. cinnamon

Mix all ingredients with blender at medium speed until
completely well mixed. (Approximately 1¹/₂ - 2 minutes). Pour
batter into a 9" x 13" cake pan that's been sprayed with a non-
fat cooking spray. Bake 35 minutes at 350 degrees.

Glaze frosting:
    ¹/₂ cup brown sugar (either light or dark)
    ¹/₂ cup powdered sugar
    5 Tbs. applesauce
    ¹/₂ tsp. cinnamon

Add all ingredients together, mix well with blender.
Immediately, once cake is removed from oven, spread glaze
frosting over top of cake while the cake is still warm-hot.

Let cake cool completely before covering. Refrigerate cake.
Good served either chilled or at room temperature.

Yield: 15 servings   Calories: 169
                              Fat: 2 grams

♥ *Blueberry Cake* ♥ *Kids Cookin'*

1 cup blueberry pie filling
1 angel food cake mix (I use Pillsbury 16 oz.)

Preheat oven to 350 degrees. Mix pie filling and angel food
cake mix together.

Spray 9" x 13" pan with non-fat cooking spray.

Bake at 350 degrees for 27 - 28 minutes. Cake will be done
when top is deep golden brown and cracks appear on the top.
Cool completely. Serve with a little dab of remaining pie filling
if desired.

Also great as a snack cake type finger food.
Yield: 20 servings   Calories: 102 per servings (Cake Only)
                        Fat: .008 (that's practically nothing!)

♥♥♥♥♥♥♥♥♥♥♥♥♥♥♥♥♥♥♥♥♥♥♥♥♥♥

♥♥♥♥♥♥♥♥♥♥♥♥♥♥♥♥♥♥♥♥♥♥♥♥♥♥♥♥♥

♥ *Frozen Chocolate Cherry Cordial Cake* ♥

Our family loves the frozen yogurt cakes that can be bought at specialty stores, but with the high cost of them I learned to make my own. They're fast to create: A huge hit every time!

99 chocolate chips
13 maraschino cherries
½ gallon fat-free frozen chocolate yogurt-softened
6 fudge cream wafers (I use Dutch Twin Reduced brand -
    5 grams fat—130 calories)

Topping:
33 chocolate chips
1 Tbs. Hershey's Chocolate Syrup
5 maraschino cherries - cut into ½'s - optional

Grind wafers in blender for a few seconds, until finely crumbled. Spray an 8" cheese cake pan (where sides of pan can release if desired) with a non-fat cooking spray. Evenly sprinkle finely crumbled wafer crumbs on bottom of pan. Do not press crumbs!

Take the 99 chocolate chips and the 13 cherries and chop into tiny pieces. (A food processor or blender will work fine for this.)

In a large bowl, stir chopped chocolate chips and cherries into softened frozen chocolate yogurt until well mixed.

Spread frozen yogurt mixture evenly over wafer crumbs.

Arrange remaining 33 chocolate chips and maraschino cherries - ¼'s (if desired) on top of cake.

Drizzle with 1 Tbs. of chocolate syrup. Freeze for 2 hours. (Takes 1 hour to set.) Keep in freezer until ready to use.

Yield: 12 servings   Calories: 184
                                Fat: 3.6 grams

♥♥♥♥♥♥♥♥♥♥♥♥♥♥♥♥♥♥♥♥♥♥♥♥♥♥♥♥♥

♥♥♥♥♥♥♥♥♥♥♥♥♥♥♥♥♥♥♥♥♥♥♥♥♥♥♥♥

♥ *Banana Split Cake* ♥

1 - 20 oz. can crushed pineapple in its own juices - no
   sugar added
1 - 18.25 oz. box lite yellow cake mix (I use Betty Crocker
   Super Moist)

On medium speed mix the whole can of crushed pineapple
with its juices with cake mix for 2-3 minutes until well mixed.
Pour cake mix into a 9" x 13" pan that's been sprayed with a
non-fat cooking spray. Bake at 350 degrees for 40 minutes, or
until toothpick put into the center of cake comes out clean. Let
cool. Once cake is completely cooled, finish cake.

Topping:
   2 Tbs. Nutra-Sweet® Spoonful™ (OR 2 tbs. sugar)
   1 can lite cherry pie filling
   2 bananas - thinly sliced
   1 8 oz. Lite Cool Whip
   2 Tbs. Hershey's Chocolate Syrup

In bowl mix 2 Tbs. Nutra-Sweet® Spoonful™ well with pie
filling. Spread cherry pie filling over completely cooled cake.
Press banana slices lightly into pie filling. Spread Lite Cool
Whip over bananas. With spoon drizzle chocolate syrup over
Cool Whip. Keep chilled until ready to serve.

Yield: 15 servings
                    With Nutra-Sweet® Spoonful™: Calories: 236
                                        Fat: 4.53 grams
            With sugar: Calories: 242   Fat: 4.53 grams

WOULDN'T IT BE NICE IF WE HAD "HINDSIGHT"
BEFORE THE FACT?

♥♥♥♥♥♥♥♥♥♥♥♥♥♥♥♥♥♥♥♥♥♥♥♥♥♥♥♥

♥ *Chocolate Cherry Chunk Frozen Cake* ♥

This dessert which appears to be painstakingly long to prepare is super easy. And just as delicious!

Kids Cookin'

Note: This is totally excellent!

1 pkg. fudge brownie mix smart size (Gold Medal)
3 Tbs. water
9 maraschino cherries - cut in ¹/₂
2 quarts cherry chocolate flake low-fat frozen yogurt (I
    used Flavorite brand) - slightly thawed
3 Healthy Choice Chocolate Sandwich Cookies

Remove creme center from cookies and discard. Crush cookies fine. (I use a blender) set aside.

With fork, stir water into brownie mix until mixture is coarse and crumbly.

Spray 8" cheese cake pan with no-fat cooking spray. Press ¹/₂ of the brownie mixture onto bottom of pan. DO NOT BAKE!!

Gently spoon slightly thawed frozen yogurt over brownie crust. With knife smooth the top of the yogurt. Add cookie crumbs to brownie crumbs. Stir until well mixed. Put on top of yogurt. Top will still look crumbly. Arrange cherry ¹/₂'s on top of crumbs. Freeze for 2 hours.

Yield: 16 servings   Calories: 230
                            Fat: 4.62 grams

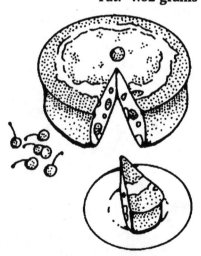

♥♥♥♥♥♥♥♥♥♥♥♥♥♥♥♥♥♥♥♥♥♥♥♥♥♥♥♥♥♥

♥ S'more Ice Cream Cake ♥ *Kids Cookin'*

Takes time to freeze.

1½ cup graham cracker crumbs
5 packets Equal® (OR ¼ c. sugar)
4 Tbs. water
2 quarts fat-free chocolate ice cream-softened
(I use Meadow Gold)
1²/₃ cup mini marshmallows
¼ cup semi-sweet chocolate chips

Mix graham cracker crumbs, Equal and water together until mixture is moist, yet crumbly. In large bowl stir together ice cream, marshmallows and chocolate chips until well blended.

Using an 8" cheese cake pan (with sides that release) press ½ of the graham cracker crumb mixture onto bottom of pan that has been sprayed with a non-fat cooking spray.

Pour ice cream mixture over crust. Evenly sprinkle remaining graham cracker crumb mixture on top of ice cream mixture.

Freeze for 2 hours or overnight.

Yield: 12 servings   With E: Calories: 207   Fat: 3.2 grams
                     With sugar: Calories: 222   Fat: 3.2 grams

♥ Marshmallow Applesauce Dessert ♥

Kids Cookin'

4 cups applesauce
¼ tsp. allspice
½ tsp. cinnamon
2 cups mini marshmallows (or quartered regular
   marshmallows)

Mix applesauce and seasonings together. Pour into a 9" x 13" pan. Sprinkle with marshmallows.

Bake at 350 degrees for 10 minutes.

Serve warm.

Yield: 15 servings   Calories: 71   Fat: 0.1 grams

**THE GIFT OF LOVE IS MORE VALUABLE THAN
ANYTHING MONEY CAN BUY.**

♥♥♥♥♥♥♥♥♥♥♥♥♥♥♥♥♥♥♥♥♥♥♥♥♥♥♥♥♥

♥♥♥♥♥♥♥♥♥♥♥♥♥♥♥♥♥♥♥♥♥♥♥♥♥

Kids Cookin' ♥ ***Brownie Dough Frozen Cake*** ♥
(Takes time to freeze)

I got this idea from cookie dough ice cream. If you like brownies and cookie dough you'll love this creation. It's one of my favorites. Beware! It's rich and filling even though low in fats.

- 1 pkg. fudge brownie mix - 10 serving size. I use Gold Medal brand - smart size package. (10.25 oz.) (If you want to use a large size brand, portion out 10 serving size and bake the rest for brownies.)
- 3 Tbs. Smucker's Fat-Free Hot Fudge
- 3 Tbs. water
- 2 quarts Swiss chocolate almond low-fat frozen yogurt (I used Flavorite brand)

—Set frozen yogurt out to soften while preparing crust.
—Mix water with brownie mix.
—Spray 8" cheesecake pan with non-fat cooking spray. (A cheesecake pan is one that the sides pop off for easier serving) If you don't have a cheesecake pan, a pie pan will work fine.

Press ²/₃ of brownie mix onto bottom of pan. (Using a fork sprayed with non-fat cooking spray works well.) DO NOT BAKE! Set aside.

—Put frozen yogurt in large bowl.
—With fingers put marble size pieces of the remaining brownie dough into frozen yogurt. Gently stir into frozen yogurt.
—Smooth frozen yogurt/brownie mixture into pan over brownie dough.
—Microwave 3 tablespoons of fat-free hot fudge. Drizzle over cake.

Freeze for 2 hours or until set.

Dip knife into hot water. Run knife along edge of pan. Take side off of pan. Cut into 12 wedges.

Yield: 12 servings

Calories: 177
Fat: 5.6 grams

IF YOU'RE TOO BUSY TO TAKE CARE OF YOURSELF,
THEN YOU'RE TOO BUSY!

♥♥♥♥♥♥♥♥♥♥♥♥♥♥♥♥♥♥♥♥♥♥♥♥♥

♥♥♥♥♥♥♥♥♥♥♥♥♥♥♥♥♥♥♥♥♥♥♥♥♥♥♥

♥ Cranberry Cake ♥ *Kids Cookin'*

*Great served warm with a dab of Lite Cool Whip or
chilled as a snack cake.*

1 super moist yellow cake mix (I used Betty Crocker brand
    with pudding in the mix.)
1 can (16 oz.) jellied cranberry sauce (I use Ocean Spray
    brand.)

Preheat oven to 350 degrees.

Spray 9" x 13" pan with non-fat cooking spray. Set aside. Set
aside ½ cup of the boxed cake mix.

With blender mix together cranberry sauce and cake mix on low
speed. Once well mixed increase speed to high. Beat on high for
2 minutes.

Spread smoothly into prepared pan. Sprinkle with remaining
½ cup dry cake mix on top.

Bake at 350 degrees for 30-32 minutes or until top is golden
brown.

Yield: 15 servings   Calories: 179   Fat: 2.4 grams

♥ Pistachio Nut Snack Cake ♥

2 boxes sugar-free pistachio pudding (4 serving size)
8 egg whites
1 box lite white cake mix (I use Lovin' Lites Pillsbury
    brand)
1 cup applesauce
1 cup water

Beat applesauce, egg whites and water on high for 30 seconds.
Add pudding and cake mix. Beat on medium speed for 2
minutes.

Spray three 8" cake pans with a non-fat cooking spray. Pour
batter evenly into pans. Bake at 350 degrees for 30 minutes.

Yield: 15 servings   Calories: 242   Fat: 2.73 grams

If desired frost with prepared Dream Whip or eat without
topping as a snack cake.

♥♥♥♥♥♥♥♥♥♥♥♥♥♥♥♥♥♥♥♥♥♥♥♥♥♥♥

♥♥♥♥♥♥♥♥♥♥♥♥♥♥♥♥♥♥♥♥♥♥♥♥♥♥♥♥

♥ Brownie Melt-A-Ways ♥

*Brownie is the nickname of our youngest child. I named these after her.
The marshmallows were her idea.*

1 - 21.5 oz. Betty Crocker Fudge Brownie Mix
5 oz. miniature marshmallows
3 Tbs. water
3 egg whites

Mix brownie mix, egg whites and water. Spray jellyroll pan
with non-fat spray. Spread mixture thinly on pan. Press
marshmallows onto mixture.

Bake at 350 degrees for 15 minutes. The tips of marshmallows
will be toasty brown. Cool and cut into 48 little squares. Store
in refrigerator.

Yield: 48 servings   Calories: 34   Fat: 0.4 grams

♥ Creamy Fat-free Chocolate Frosting ♥

$^3/_4$ cup fat-free Ultra Promise margarine
$3^1/_2$ - 4 cups powdered sugar
$^3/_4$ cup cocoa
1 tsp. vanilla
4 - 5 packets Equal® (OR 3 tbs. more powdered sugar)

Beat all ingredients together until smooth and creamy. If you
want a creamier frosting, use more fat-free Promise. If you
want a stiffer frosting, add more powdered sugar.

Yield: 24 servings
                    With Equal®: Calories: 87   Fat: 0.4 grams
                    With sugar only: Calories: 91   Fat: 0.4 grams

♥♥♥♥♥♥♥♥♥♥♥♥♥♥♥♥♥♥♥♥♥♥♥♥♥♥♥

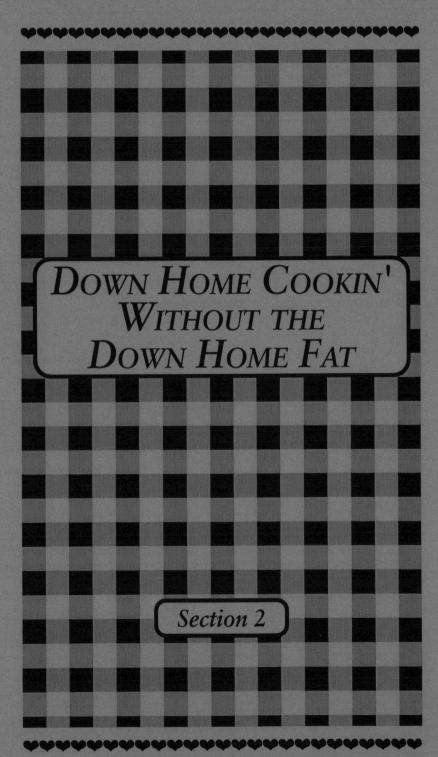

DOWN HOME COOKIN'
WITHOUT THE
DOWN HOME FAT

Section 2

*Write your personal notes and
names of favorite recipes here.*

Appetizers
Snacks
Beverages

Mini Contents

(Appetizers, Snacks, Beverage)

♥♥♥♥♥♥♥♥♥♥♥♥♥♥♥♥♥♥♥♥♥♥♥♥♥

♥ *"Yum to your Tum" Appetizers* ♥

8 oz. fat-free cream cheese (I use Healthy Choice) *Kids Cookin'*
3 Tbs. chunky salsa
1 Tbs. + 1 tsp. reduced calorie Hidden Valley Ranch Salad
   Dressing mix-dry
10 fat-free flour tortillas (I like Buena Vista brand)
4 cups lettuce - finely chopped
1 cup salsa for dipping (if desired)

Note: You will use 5 flour tortillas for each stack. Then you
will cut each stack into 12 pieces of pie.

Mix first 3 ingredients until well blended. Spread about 2$\frac{1}{2}$
Tbs. of cream mixture on tortilla. Top with $\frac{1}{2}$ cup finely
chopped lettuce. Repeat this process 3 more times. Top with
5th tortilla. With hands press top firmly down.

Cut like a pie into 12 pieces. If desired, when eating use salsa
for dipping.

If you like a spicier appetizer, add 1 tsp. Tabasco sauce to
cream mixture.

Yield: 24 servings   Calories: 60   Fat: 0 grams

THE ONLY PERSON YOU NEED TO PLEASE IN LIFE IS
YOURSELF AND GOD. THOSE ARE THE ONLY TWO YOU
ARE ACCOUNTABLE TO.

♥♥♥♥♥♥♥♥♥♥♥♥♥♥♥♥♥♥♥♥♥♥♥♥♥

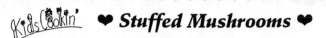

❤ *Stuffed Mushrooms* ❤

$^1/_2$ cup Italian style bread crumbs
1 cup turkey ham - finely chopped
$^1/_2$ cup onion - finely chopped
1 tsp. garlic powder
pinch of ground sage
1 Tbs. Ultra fat-free Promise Margarine
1 Tbs. grated Parmesan cheese
12 - 14 large fresh mushrooms - cleaned - with stems
    taken out
Molly McButter Sour Cream flavored powdered substitute

Spray skillet with non-fat cooking spray. Brown onions and ham for a couple of minutes. Add fat-free Promise, garlic and sage. Stir until well blended. Remove from heat. Add bread crumbs and Parmesan cheese.

With fingers stuff each prepared mushroom cap. Sprinkle with sour cream flavored substitute.

Bake at 350 degrees for 20 minutes. Serve warm.

Yield: 7 servings   **Calories: 74**   **Fat: 1.6**

THE BEST REMEDY FOR DISCONTENTMENT IS TO LOOK AT ALL WE HAVE TO BE THANKFUL FOR.

♥♥♥♥♥♥♥♥♥♥♥♥♥♥♥♥♥♥♥♥♥♥♥♥♥♥♥♥

♥ *Ham & Onion Roll-ups* ♥ *Kids Cookin'*

1 pkg. reduced calorie Hidden Valley Ranch Salad Dressing
  Mix - dry
1 packet Equal® (OR 2 tsp. sugar)
³/₄ cup no-fat cottage cheese
4 oz. fat-free cream cheese
³/₄ cup no-fat sour cream
3 Tbs. water
1 slice very thin ham (I use Oscar Mayer Deli Thin)
1 fresh green onion

Beat cottage cheese on high for 1-2 minutes until smooth and creamy. Add everything but ham and onion. Beat on medium until well blended.

Spread a thin layer of vegetable dip on ham. Starting from the smallest part of ham slice, roll the green onion up with the ham.

If you'd like, you can slice the long ham/onion roll-up into ¹/₃ or ¹/₂ and place on fat-free Health Valley Crackers.

Serving size: 2 pieces (not cut)
> With Equal®: Calories: 48   Fat: 1 gram
> With sugar: Calories: 52   Fat: 1 gram

♥ *Spinach Balls* (The Healthy Ones!) ♥
Great as an appetizer or a side dish with pork.

2 pkg. frozen chopped spinach - drained
1 pkg. stove top stuffing with seasoning
1¹/₂ cups Egg Beaters or 12 egg whites
1 tsp. garlic powder
³/₄ cup melted butter buds or fat-free Ultra Promise
  Margarine
1 onion - chopped
¹/₄ cup Parmesan cheese

Mix thawed spinach and stuffing - set aside. Mix the rest of the ingredients together, then mix both mixtures together. Chill. Form into balls.

Bake at 350 degrees for 20 minutes on a cookie sheet that has been sprayed with a non-fat cooking spray.

Yield: 12 servings as a side dish   Calories: 89   Fat: 1.6 grams
      OR 24 appetizers   Calories: 45   Fat: 0.8 grams

♥♥♥♥♥♥♥♥♥♥♥♥♥♥♥♥♥♥♥♥♥♥♥♥♥♥♥♥

♥♥♥♥♥♥♥♥♥♥♥♥♥♥♥♥♥♥♥♥♥♥♥♥♥♥♥

♥ Julie Casillas's Mexican Dip ♥

Kids Cookin'

1 can Health Valley fat-free chili w/beans (I find this at
Kroger's)
2 - 8 oz. pkgs. fat-free cream cheese

Mix together, put in crockpot, heat and serve.

Optional: Salsa
Chopped onions

Serve with your favorite brand of low-fat tortilla chips.

Without chips—
Yield 12 - 3 oz. servings   Calories: 39
Fat: 0 grams

♥ Vegetable Pizza ♥

2 cans Rightshape Biscuits (20 biscuits total)

Knead dough. On floured surface roll dough out. Spray a
cookie sheet with edges (15" x 9¼") with a non-fat cooking
spray. Press dough out onto cookie sheet covering whole
sheet. With fork poke holes all over through the dough. Bake
at 425 degrees for 7-9 minutes, until golden brown.

¹/₂ cup fat-free sour cream
¹/₂ cup fat-free mayonnaise
8 oz. fat-free cream cheese - softened
1 - 1.1 oz. size packet of Hidden Valley Ranch reduced
calorie Salad Dressing Mix

Beat at medium speed until well mixed. Spread mixture onto
crust, covering all the way to the sides. Cover with your
favorite fresh, chopped vegetables. I like red peppers, green
peppers, mushrooms, broccoli, carrots, cherry tomatoes and
celery.

Yield: 35 servings   Calories: 50   Fat: 28 grams

♥♥♥♥♥♥♥♥♥♥♥♥♥♥♥♥♥♥♥♥♥♥♥♥♥♥♥

Breads
Rolls
Muffins

Mini Contents

(Breads, Rolls, Muffins)

♥♥♥♥♥♥♥♥♥♥♥♥♥♥♥♥♥♥♥♥♥♥♥♥♥♥♥♥

♥ *Mmm! Ma! Ma! Mi Ya Bread!* ♥

Great with Italian food.

1 pkg. yeast
1¹/₂ cups warm water
1 tsp. salt
1 Tbs. sugar
2 cups whole wheat flour
2 cups self-rising flour
2 tsp. oregano (1 tsp. per pan)
2 tsp. basil (1 tsp. per pan)
2 tsp. garlic salt (1 tsp. per pan)
¹/₂ cup liquid Butter Buds (¹/₄ cup per pan)
¹/₂ cup grated Parmesan cheese (¹/₄ cup per pan)

Preheat oven to 425 degrees.   Makes 2 jellyroll pans.

Dissolve yeast in warm water. Add salt and sugar, stir until dissolved in the water. Add both kinds of flour to water mixture. Knead on lightly floured surface. Spray 2 jellyroll pans with non-fat spray. Divide the dough into two.

Put each dough ball into each jellyroll pan and roll out dough to edges of pan with rolling pin. Spread ¹/₄ cup of liquid Butter Buds onto each pan of dough. Sprinkle with garlic salt, basil, oregano, and Parmesan cheese.

Bake in 425 degree oven for 15-20 minutes or until crust is nice and brown.

Serve warm.

Yield: 24 servings   Calories: 81   Fat: 0.8 grams

BE A BLESSING TO OTHERS

♥♥♥♥♥♥♥♥♥♥♥♥♥♥♥♥♥♥♥♥♥♥♥♥♥♥♥♥♥♥

❤ *My Grandma Schaefer's Applebutter* ❤

This is absolutely, positively the best and easiest applebutter I have ever eaten! You haven't had applebutter till you've had this!

10 cups of cooked apples (about 12 large apples, cored)
    cook in about ¼ cup water
6 cups sugar
1 tsp. cinnamon
1 tsp. allspice
½ tsp. ground cloves

Put cooked apples in blender. Beat until all ground up. Put in crockpot for 17 hours. Stir once in a while. Take lid off for last two hours. Fill canning jar ½" shy of the top. Melt paraffin and pour over.

If you don't want to can it, just keep it refrigerated. Our family eats it up fast!

I love to eat this with fat-free cottage cheese.

Yield: 256 servings (1 Tbs. each)   Calories: 24
                                           Fat: 0 grams

ALWAYS TRY TO DO THE BEST YOU CAN WITH WHAT YOU'VE GOT.

♥♥♥♥♥♥♥♥♥♥♥♥♥♥♥♥♥♥♥♥♥♥♥♥♥♥

♥ *Yummy Whole Wheat Pretzels* ♥

These are fun to make with your children! I really enjoy it!
Rather than just making pretzel shapes only, our children and I like to
make unique and fun shapes such as hearts, balloon, a kiss, etc. Be
creative and have fun!

Kids Cookin'

2 pkg. yeast
3 cups warm water
2 tsp. salt (coarse salt if desired)
2 Tbs. sugar
5 cups whole wheat flour
3 cups self rising flour
2 egg whites - beaten

Dissolve 2 pkgs. of yeast in 3 cups of warm water. Add salt
and sugar to water and stir until dissolved. Add both kinds of
flour. Stir until combined. Knead on lightly floured surface.
Separate into 36 individual balls. Roll each ball between
hands until dough is long enough to make into a large pretzel.
(12-15 inches). Brush with beaten egg whites, after the pretzel
has been placed on a cookie sheet that has been sprayed with
a non-fat spray.

If desired, sprinkle lightly with coarse salt. Bake for 10-12
minutes or until the tips of pretzels are slightly brown.

Yield: 36 servings   Calories: 94   Fat: 0.4

**SOME THINGS ARE BETTER LEFT UNSAID
— LIKE YOUR WEIGHT AND YOUR AGE.**

♥♥♥♥♥♥♥♥♥♥♥♥♥♥♥♥♥♥♥♥♥♥♥♥♥♥

♥♥♥♥♥♥♥♥♥♥♥♥♥♥♥♥♥♥♥♥♥♥♥♥♥♥

♥ *Cinnamon Oatmeal Muffins* ♥

1 pkg. white Lovin' Lites cake mix
2 Tbs. cinnamon
¹/₂ cup oatmeal
1¹/₂ cups water
4 egg whites

Mix together well. Pour into prepared muffin tins that have
been sprayed with a non-fat cooking spray.

Crumb topping:
1 Tbs. cinnamon
3 Tbs. whole wheat flour
4 Tbs. oatmeal
¹/₂ cup dark brown sugar
2 Tbs. no-fat margarine (I use Ultra Promise fat-free)

With fork mix until dry and crumbly. With fingers sprinkle on
top of muffin batter already in tins.

Bake 25 minutes at 350 degrees.

Yield: 12 servings   Calories: 188   Fat: 2.9
       18 servings   Calories: 125   Fat: 1.9

LIKE YOURSELF.

♥♥♥♥♥♥♥♥♥♥♥♥♥♥♥♥♥♥♥♥♥♥♥♥♥♥

♥♥♥♥♥♥♥♥♥♥♥♥♥♥♥♥♥♥♥♥♥♥♥♥♥♥♥♥♥♥

♥ *Very Berry Muffins* ♥

1 cup your favorite berries
1¹/₂ cups whole wheat flour
2 cups all purpose flour
1¹/₂ Tbs. Nutra-Sweet® Spoonful™ (<u>OR</u> 1¹/₂ Tbs. sugar)
5 tsp. baking powder
2 tsp. lite salt
1¹/₂ cups water
²/₃ cup applesauce
4 egg whites (beat just until foamy)
4 Tbs. sugar
your favorite berry preserves

Beat egg whites with mixer until foamy. Add remaining ingredients. By hand stir just until moistened. Batter will be lumpy. Carefully fold berries into batter.

Spray muffin tins with a non-fat cooking spray. Fill cups ²/₃ full. Put 2 tsp. raspberry (or your favorite berry) preserves on top of batter in each muffin cup before baking.

Bake at 400 degrees for 20 minutes. (Longer for larger muffins)

Yield: 12 servings
  With Nutra-Sweet® Spoonful™: Calories: 163 Fat: 0.5 grams
  With sugar: Calories: 169   Fat: 0.5 grams

I'D RATHER HAVE A MESSY HOME
FILLED WITH FRIENDS IN IT,
THAN A CLEAN HOME AND NO FRIENDS IN IT.

SO MY HOME IS USUALLY MESSY,
BUT IT'S FILLED WITH FRIENDS!

♥♥♥♥♥♥♥♥♥♥♥♥♥♥♥♥♥♥♥♥♥♥♥♥♥♥♥♥♥

♥♥♥♥♥♥♥♥♥♥♥♥♥♥♥♥♥♥♥♥♥♥♥♥♥♥♥♥

♥ *Pumpkin Muffins* ♥

1 cup liquid Butter Buds
2 cups brown sugar
$^1/_3$ cup Sugar Twin brown sugar replacement
8 egg whites
1 tsp. of each - cinnamon, nutmeg, lite salt
1 cup canned pumpkin
$^2/_3$ cup water
2 tsp. baking soda
2 cups whole wheat flour
1 cup flour

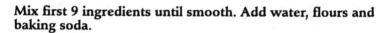

Mix first 9 ingredients until smooth. Add water, flours and baking soda.

Spray muffin tins with a no-fat cooking spray. Using Nutra-Sweet coat insides of muffin tins as you would with flour. Fill tins up to rim with batter.

Crumb topping:
    1 Tbs. dry Butter Buds
    1 Tbs. sugar
    1 tsp. brown sugar
    1 tsp. flour
    1 tsp. cinnamon
    4 tsp. water

With fork mix all ingredients listed above until crumbly. Sprinkle topping on muffins before baking. Lightly sprinkle Nutra-Sweet on top of crumb topping.

Bake at 350 degrees. Mini muffins 30-35 minutes
                      Large muffins 40-45 minutes
    Bake until knife inserted in center comes out clean.

Good served warm.

Serving size: 1 muffin   Calories: (approximate) Mini - 50
                                        Large - 200

IF YOU DON'T WANT TO PUCKER,
DON'T EAT SOUR LEMONS.

♥♥♥♥♥♥♥♥♥♥♥♥♥♥♥♥♥♥♥♥♥♥♥♥♥♥♥♥

❤ *Bran Banana Muffins* ❤

1³/₄ cups whole wheat flour
2 tsp. baking powder
¹/₂ tsp. ground cloves
¹/₂ tsp. lite salt
¹/₄ cup oat bran
¹/₂ cup Nabisco 100% Bran cereal
4 egg whites
¹/₃ cup water
1 pkg. Butter Buds - dry
4 medium ripe bananas - mashed

Soak bran cereal in water, until moist. Add egg whites. Mix together well. Add remaining ingredients. Mix until all is blended. Put mixture into desired size muffin pans, that have been sprayed with a non-fat cooking spray.

Topping:
¹/₃ cup flour
¹/₃ cup sugar
1 pkg. Butter Buds - dry
1 tsp. vanilla
1-to-2 tsp. water (just enough to make topping crumbly)

Mix topping with fork until coarse and crumbly. Sprinkle, with fingers, on top of batter already in pan.

Bake at 350 degrees. Bake depending on muffin tin size.
Mini -approximately 15 minutes.
Regular - approximately 25-30 minutes.
Large - approximately 35-40 minutes.
Bake until knife inserted in middle comes out clean.

Yield: 12 servings   Calories: 104   Fat: 0.7

THE BIBLE TEACHES US TO TREAT OTHERS
THE WAY WE WANT TO BE TREATED.
THE PROBLEM IS THAT MANY OF US TREAT
OTHERS BETTER THAN WE TREAT OURSELVES.

Soups
Salads
Vegetables

Mini Contents

(Soups, Salads, Vegetables)

♥♥♥♥♥♥♥♥♥♥♥♥♥♥♥♥♥♥♥♥♥♥♥♥

♥ *Beef Barley Soup* ♥

    1 lb. ground eye of round (beef)
    2 medium onions - diced
    4 medium tomatoes - diced
    2 Tbs. garlic salt
    1 Tbs. fresh basil

In a large dutch oven brown beef. Do not drain. Add onions, tomatoes, garlic salt and basil. Cook over medium heat for 5 minutes.

Add:
    12 cups water
    16 oz. bag of frozen mixed vegetables (carrots, peas, corn, green beans and lima beans)
    4 bay leaves
    1 tsp. Worcestershire Sauce
    1/2 tsp. black pepper
    1 - 11 oz. box of quick cooking barley

Bring to a boil. Reduce heat. Let simmer at least 10-15 minutes. The longer it simmers the more flavorful it gets. (I think).

Remove bay leaves before serving.

Yield: 21 servings   Calories: 114   Fat: 1.8

♥ *"Pink Cadillac" Jello Salad* ♥

    1 box of strawberry sugar-free Jello (4 servings size)
    20 oz. can of crushed pineapple in its juices
    1 cup fat-free cottage cheese
    1 cup lite Cool Whip
    1 fresh strawberry to garnish - if desired

Heat crushed pineapple to a boil. Add strawberry Jello. Remove from heat and stir well. Cool. Then add cottage cheese and lite Cool Whip. Pour into medium size serving bowl.

Cut 3 slices 1/2 way through the fresh strawberry and with fingers, open strawberry into a fan shape. Place on top of Jello for a pretty garnish if desired.

Yield: 13 servings   Calories: 52   Fat: .77 grams

♥♥♥♥♥♥♥♥♥♥♥♥♥♥♥♥♥♥♥♥♥♥♥♥

♥♥♥♥♥♥♥♥♥♥♥♥♥♥♥♥♥♥♥♥♥♥♥♥♥♥

♥ *Cream of Mushroom and Broccoli Soup* ♥

16 oz. fat-free plain yogurt
2 bunches of fresh broccoli-chopped, or a 2 lb. bag frozen
    broccoli
1 cup cornstarch
4 cups fresh mushrooms - sliced thin
8 oz. fat-free shredded Cheddar cheese
2 onions - chopped
1 Tbs. lite salt
2 pkgs. Butter Buds - dry
3 quarts skim milk
1¹/₂ cups carrots - grated
1 Tbs. garlic salt
¹/₄ tsp. pepper

Cook broccoli in microwave until tender. Sauté onions and mushrooms with dry Butter Buds with garlic salt and pepper for about 5 minutes on low heat until onions are tender. Add chopped broccoli. Sauté 15 minutes. Add milk and cornstarch. Simmer until thickened - about ¹/₂ hour.

Yield: 24 servings (1 cup each)   Calories: 56
                                          Fat: 0.1

♥ *Mashed Potato Bake* ♥

6 cups boiled potatoes - peeled and cubed
12 oz. fat-free cottage cheese
1 envelope Butter Buds
1 small onion-finely chopped (¹/₂ cup)
1 tsp. lite salt-optional
1 Tbs. chopped parsley-if desired-optional
1 Tbs. pepper to taste- if desired-optional

In medium size bowl, with mixer, beat all ingredients on medium to high for 3-4 minutes.

Spray a 9" x 13" pan with a non-fat cooking spray. Bake at 350 degrees for 30-35 minutes. Top may be lightly browned.

Yield: 15-1/2 cup servings   Calories: 65   Fat: 0 grams

**ALWAYS TRY TO DO THE BEST YOU CAN WITH WHAT
YOU'VE GOT.**

♥♥♥♥♥♥♥♥♥♥♥♥♥♥♥♥♥♥♥♥♥♥♥♥♥♥

♥ Carrot & Lentil Soup ♥

A hearty, stick to your bones, high protein soup!!!
Great for a cup of soup before a meal, soup and salad for lunch, or as a
meal with corn bread. (A great source of protein and fiber)

        1 lb. lentils
        8 cups water

Put lentils and water in large pot. Bring to a rapid boil; boil for
2 minutes. Reduce heat to a simmer. Add the following
ingredients, cover and simmer for at least 2 hours. (Until
carrots and lentils are tender.) Stir occasionally.

Add:
        4 cups sliced carrots
        1 medium onion, finely chopped
        46 oz. can of V-8 Juice
        28 oz. can crushed tomatoes - concentrated
        1 tsp. Liquid Smoke-Hickory Seasoning (found in Bar-B-
            Que sauce section of grocery store)
        2 bay leaves
        1 Tbs. plus 1 tsp. garlic salt
        2 tsp. Nutra-Sweet® Spoonful™ (OR 1½ Tbs. sugar)

Yield: 19 - 1 cup servings
    With Nutra-Sweet® Spoonful™: Calories: 121   Fat: .61 grams
    With sugar: Calories: 123   Fat: .61 grams

WRITING A BOOK IS A LOT LIKE HAVING A BABY—YOU
HOPE IT IS GOING TO BE GOOD AND A BLESSING TO
OTHERS.

♥♥♥♥♥♥♥♥♥♥♥♥♥♥♥♥♥♥♥♥♥♥♥♥♥♥

♥ *Chicken Poppie Soup* ♥

1 lb. raw skinless chicken breast - cut into bite sized pieces
6 oz. box Stove Top Stuffing - chicken flavor
1 packet Butter Buds - dry
2 cups water
1 box (¹/₄ oz. size) Knorr Vegetable Soup Mix - dry
46 oz. size can of clear chicken broth (remove fat floating
    on top of broth)
2¹/₂ - 3 cups flour
46 oz. water (fill empty chicken broth can once)

In a bowl add 2 cups water to Stove Top Stuffing Mix,
(croutons and seasoning packet) along with 1 packet Butter
Buds and stir. Set aside for 5 minutes.

In large soup pan put raw chicken, 46 oz. clear chicken broth,
box of dry vegetable soup mix and 46 oz. water over medium
- high heat. Bring to a boil.

While soup is coming to a boil add 1¹/₂ cups of flour to the
bowl of stuffing. Mix together well. (It's easier if you add ¹/₂
cup at a time). On floured surface put stuffing mixture.
Sprinkle flour on top of stuffing so that you can press dough
out into ¹/₂" thickness. With knife cut dough into ³/₄" - 1"
pieces. Drop cut dough pieces into boiling soup. Let boil 7
minutes. Dough pieces will be thoroughly cooked and kind of
stiff when done. Serve hot.

Yield: 14-1 cup servings   Calories: 201
                                   Fat: 3.64 grams

♥♥♥♥♥♥♥♥♥♥♥♥♥♥♥♥♥♥♥♥♥♥♥♥♥♥

❤❤❤❤❤❤❤❤❤❤❤❤❤❤❤❤❤❤❤❤❤❤❤❤❤❤

❤ *My Mom's Augratin Soup* ❤
Easy to put together and absolutely delicious!

3 boxes augratin potatoes (your favorite brand) - set
    cheese aside
1 head cauliflower - fresh
1 bunch broccoli -
1 packet onion soup mix - dry

Put all in a 6 quart Dutch Oven. Cover with water
(approximately 4^1/$_2$ quarts), until all ingredients are covered.
Bring to a boil, reduce heat and simmer until tender, about 20-
30 minutes.

Add:
    1^1/$_2$ quart skim milk
    1 tsp. rubbed thyme - dried
    1 tsp. marjoram leaves - dried
    2 tsp. parsley
    3 packets of cheese from the boxed potatoes
    8 slices fat-free American cheese

If it's not as thick as you would like it, add 2 tsp. cornstarch
with a ^{1}/$_4$ cup milk.

Salt and pepper to taste. If desired, add thinly chopped turkey
ham.

Yield: 30 (approx. 1 cup) servings   Calories: 94
                                          Fat: 0.5

❤ *Orange Cranberry Jello Salad* ❤

1 - 4 oz. can Mandarin oranges - drained
1 - 16 oz. can jellied cranberry sauce
1 - 4 serving size orange Jello - sugar free
1 cup boiling water

Add 1 cup boiling water to Jello. Stir for 2 minutes. Add jellied
cranberries, stir. Once dissolved, add oranges.

Refrigerate overnight or 2 hours. Serve chilled.

Yield: 7 servings (4 oz. each ^{1}/$_2$ cup each)   Calories: 21
                                                            Fat: 0 grams

❤❤❤❤❤❤❤❤❤❤❤❤❤❤❤❤❤❤❤❤❤❤❤❤❤

♥♥♥♥♥♥♥♥♥♥♥♥♥♥♥♥♥♥♥♥♥♥♥♥♥♥♥

♥ *Crunchy Sunshine Salad* ♥

As a child this was my favorite Jello salad.

1 orange flavored sugar-free Jello gelatin (8 serving size)
1^1/$_2$ cups boiling water
1 cup diet Sprite
^{3}/$_4$ cup finely chopped fresh carrots
^{3}/$_4$ cup finely chopped fresh celery
^{1}/$_4$ cup finely chopped pecans (or walnuts)
1 cup no-fat ricotta cheese (I like Frigo brand)
1 - 20 oz. can crushed pineapple (drain juice!)
1 - 11 oz. Mandarin orange segments - drained (optional)

Dissolve Jello gelatin in large bowl with boiling water. Stir for 2 minutes. Add diet Sprite, carrots, celery, pecans, drained pineapple and no-fat ricotta cheese. Stir until ricotta cheese is almost completely dissolved. Pour into individual glass cups, a pretty jello mold or a pretty bowl.

Refrigerate about 1 hour until firm. Drain juice from Mandarin orange segments. Arrange orange segments in flowers on top of Jello before serving. (Optional)

For a special treat, if you don't have pretty dessert cups, spoon into wine glasses.

Yield: 9 servings   Calories: 95 (w/oranges) Fat: 2.25 grams

♥ *Honey Dijon Salad Dressing* ♥

Excellent for potato salad and also "Summer Fiesta!" salad.

^{3}/$_4$ cup Kraft Free Miracle Whip
^{3}/$_4$ cup Kraft Free Mayonnaise
^{1}/$_4$ cup Dijon mustard
^{1}/$_3$ cup apple cider vinegar
1 tsp. garlic salt
^{1}/$_4$ cup brown sugar
^{1}/$_4$ cup honey
^{1}/$_2$ cup plus 2 tsp. water

In a microwave safe bowl heat honey, brown sugar and water until dissolved, approximately 30 seconds. Add rest of ingredients. Beat on high with blender until thoroughly mixed.

Yield: 24 servings (2 Tbs. each) Calories: 29   Fat: 0.1 grams

♥♥♥♥♥♥♥♥♥♥♥♥♥♥♥♥♥♥♥♥♥♥♥♥♥♥♥

♥♥♥♥♥♥♥♥♥♥♥♥♥♥♥♥♥♥♥♥♥♥♥♥♥♥♥♥

♥ *Chicken Caesar Salad* ♥

This is by far my family's favorite salad!!!

2 heads Romaine lettuce - cleaned and torn into bite size
    pieces
4 chicken breasts
$^1/_2$ cup finely shredded Parmesan cheese
pepper - optional
fat-free croutons - optional
1 c. fat-free Caesar Dressing (I like Hidden Valley's brand)

Toss lettuce with Caesar dressing in large bowl.
Cook chicken breast on grill. Slice into thin strips.
Divide salad onto 4 plates. Top with chicken strips. Garnish
with shredded Parmesan cheese, fat-free croutons and ground
pepper if desired.
Best when salad is chilled and chicken is hot off the grill.
This salad is excellent without the chicken also.

♥ *Vegetable Jello Salad* ♥

*This recipe is a sneaky way to make sure your
children eat their vegetables!
This vegetable Jello salad is great with chicken!*

1 pkg. lemon sugar-free Jello (4 serving size)
1 pkg. orange sugar-free Jello (4 serving size)
1 tsp. vinegar (I use apple cider vinegar)
4 cups water
1 cup celery-finely chopped
2 cups carrots-shredded
1 can crushed pineapple-in its own juices
8 Tbs. Kraft "Free" Miracle Whip

In saucepan bring 4 cups of water and the whole can of
pineapple, with its juices, to a boil. Remove from heat. Add
both lemon and orange jello. Let cool a couple of minutes.
Add celery, vinegar and carrots. Pour into a 9" x 13" pan. Let
sit overnight or at least 4 hours. With a knife smooth on
"Free" Miracle Whip.

Yield: 15 servings   Calories: 41   Fat: 0 grams

HANG AROUND QUALITY PEOPLE.

♥♥♥♥♥♥♥♥♥♥♥♥♥♥♥♥♥♥♥♥♥♥♥♥♥♥♥♥

❤❤❤❤❤❤❤❤❤❤❤❤❤❤❤❤❤❤❤❤❤❤❤❤❤❤

❤ *California Sunshine (Salad)* ❤

1 lb. spaghetti cooked, drained and cooled
10 slices honey roasted & smoked turkey breast lunchmeat
   - diced
1 lb. California blend frozen vegetables - thawed (carrots,
   broccoli and cauliflower)
1 medium sweet onion - chopped

Dressing:
   ¹/₂ cup rice vinegar
   1 tsp. Nutra-Sweet® Spoonful™ (<u>OR</u> 1 tsp. sugar)
   2 tsp. ginger
   ¹/₃ cup water
   ¹/₂ tsp. poppyseed

Mix dressing ingredients all together. Pour over salad.

Serve chilled. (Salt and pepper to taste)

Yield: 16 servings
   With Nutra-Sweet® Spoonful™: Calories: 96   Fat: 2.5 grams
   With Sugar: Calories: 97   Fat: 2.5 grams

❤ *Large Shrimp Sunshine Salad* ❤

3 - 4 cups lettuce (your favorite kinds) cleaned and cut into
   bite size pieces
¹/₂ cup Marzetti Fat-Free Sweet and Sour Salad Dressing
1 cup salad shrimp - cooked and chilled
¹/₄ cup pineapple chunks (juice drained)
¹/₄ cup grated carrot

Toss all above ingredients together.

Serve chilled.

Serving size: 1   Calories: 320

❤❤❤❤❤❤❤❤❤❤❤❤❤❤❤❤❤❤❤❤❤❤❤❤❤❤

♥♥♥♥♥♥♥♥♥♥♥♥♥♥♥♥♥♥♥♥♥♥♥♥♥♥♥♥

♥ Grilled Steak and Salad ♥

This is a meal in itself! Serve with your favorite no-fat salad dressing.

3 - 4 ounces - eye of round (beef)
1 hard boiled egg white - chopped
3 cups of your favorite lettuces
¹/₄ cup chopped onion
¹/₄ cup chopped mushrooms - fresh
your favorite no-fat dressing

Grill steak to desired doneness' rare, medium or well done. Slice steak on cutting board into ¹/₄" slices while still hot. Sprinkle with garlic salt lightly (optional).

Arrange cooked, sliced steak on already prepared fresh salad that contains 3 cups of your favorite lettuces, 1 hard boiled egg white - chopped, ¹/₄ cup chopped onion and ¹/₄ cup chopped fresh mushrooms.

Yield: 1 serving without dressing

Calories: 169
Fat: 4.6 grams

♥ Festive Cranberry Pineapple Salad ♥

Great for the holidays with turkey or ham.

12 oz. fresh cranberries
¹/₂ cup Nutra-Sweet® Spoonful™ (OR ¹/₂ c. sugar)
1 - 8 oz. Lite Cool Whip
2 cups miniature marshmallows
¹/₄ cup chopped walnuts (optional)
1-20 oz. can crushed pineapple - drained

Grind cranberries in food processor for 1 minute. Pour into bowl and add all remaining ingredients. Keep chilled at least ¹/₂ a day. The longer it sits the better I think it tastes.

Yield: 14 servings (¹/₂ cup each)
  With Nutra-Sweet® Spoonful™: Calories: 114   Fat: 1.4 grams
  With sugar: Calories: 142   Fat: 1.4 grams

♥♥♥♥♥♥♥♥♥♥♥♥♥♥♥♥♥♥♥♥♥♥♥♥♥♥♥

♥♥♥♥♥♥♥♥♥♥♥♥♥♥♥♥♥♥♥♥♥♥♥♥♥♥♥

♥ Cinnamon Apple Salad ♥

A dessert or a side dish.
This recipe is especially good with chicken or pork meals.

1 cup hot water
1 tsp. cinnamon
1 envelope (box) of sugar-free strawberry Jello (4 serving
   size)
1 cup applesauce
1 cup apple with skin on - chopped into tiny pieces
1 cup chopped celery

Dissolve Jello and cinnamon in hot water, stirring constantly
until completely dissolved.

Add applesauce and stir until completely mixed. Stir in apples
and celery. Once well mixed, pour into Jello ring mold. (If you
don't want to use a mold you don't have to.)

Chill at least 2 hours.

Yield: 8-1/2 cup servings   Calories: 42   Fat: 0 grams

♥ Kermit's Salad ♥

This is a tart salad.

1 small sugar-free lime Jello (4 serving size)
1 small sugar-free lemon Jello (4 serving size)
1 cup hot water
2 cups sugar-free Mountain Dew (pop)
1 cup fat-free cottage cheese
1 cup Free Miracle Whip
1 can crushed pineapple in pineapple juice - drained
1 Tbs. finely chopped pecans - optional

Dissolve both Jello's in hot water. Once completely dissolved
add Mountain Dew. Set aside.

Drain juices from pineapple. Mix well together: pineapple,
Miracle Whip and cottage cheese. Once well blended, add to
Jello.

Refrigerate at least 3 hours before serving. Needs time to set.

Sprinkle with finely chopped nuts if desired.

Yield: 12 servings   Calories: 38   Fat: 0.4
♥♥♥♥♥♥♥♥♥♥♥♥♥♥♥♥♥♥♥♥♥♥♥♥♥♥♥

♥♥♥♥♥♥♥♥♥♥♥♥♥♥♥♥♥♥♥♥♥♥♥♥♥♥♥♥♥♥

♥ *Gourmet Chicken Salad* ♥
This is my absolute best!

2 cups cooked, cubed chicken breast - meat only
   (approximately 10 oz.)
$\frac{1}{2}$ cup apples with skin on, coarsely chopped (1 small)
25 raisins - chopped
$\frac{1}{4}$ cup celery - coarsely chopped
1 Tbs. chopped chives
$\frac{1}{2}$ cup fat-free Miracle Whip
2 tsp. sesame seeds
2 tsp. lemon juice (I use bottled lemon juice)
2 tsp. brown sugar
2 tsp. ground ginger
dash of lite salt - optional

For dressing mix together chives, fat-free Miracle Whip,
sesame seeds, lemon juice, brown sugar, ginger and lite salt, in
a medium large bowl. Mix until well blended. Add chicken
breast, apples, raisins, and celery. Toss until well covered with
dressing.

Cover and keep refrigerated until ready to eat.

Yield: 4 servings   Calories: 169   Fat: 3.25 grams

Different ways to serve Gourmet Chicken Salad:

* Use $\frac{1}{2}$ of cantaloupe or honeydew melon. Cut melon in $\frac{1}{2}$.
With spoon clean out seeds of melon. With knife cut the end
of the melon flat giving the bowl shape a flat surface to sit on.
Stuff cantaloupe with gourmet chicken salad.
* Take a seedless Navel orange and cut into $\frac{1}{8}$, not cutting all
the way through. Open like a flower. Stuff center of opened
up flower cut orange with gourmet chicken salad.
* Serve gourmet chicken salad on top of a pretty bed of
assorted freshly torn lettuce leaves.
* Serve open faced on $\frac{1}{2}$ a toasted raisin bagel.
* Serve on top of chilled pasta.

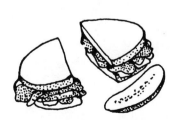

♥♥♥♥♥♥♥♥♥♥♥♥♥♥♥♥♥♥♥♥♥♥♥♥♥♥♥♥

♥♥♥♥♥♥♥♥♥♥♥♥♥♥♥♥♥♥♥♥♥♥♥♥♥♥♥

♥ *Di's Zingy Italian Pasta* ♥

8 ounces spiral pasta, cooked in unsalted water and
    drained
2 medium tomatoes, cut into wedges
1 cucumber
1 green pepper
$^1/_2$ cup fat-free Miracle Whip
$^1/_3$ cup red wine vinegar (I use a little less than $^1/_2$ cup)
1 Tbs. + $^1/_2$ tsp. sugar
2 Tbs. dry Italian Seasoning mix + 1 tsp.

In a large bowl, combine pasta, tomatoes, cucumber and green
pepper. Set aside. In a small bowl, combine mayo, vinegar,
sugar, and seasoning mix. Taste this mixture and adjust it to
your taste. Pour over salad and toss to coat well. Cover and
chill 2 hours.

Yield: 10 servings   Calories: 50   Fat: 0.5 grams

♥ *Tuna-Pasta Salad Delight* ♥

6 oz. can of tuna (in water)
8 slices no-fat American cheese - sliced into thin strips
3 egg whites - hard boiled - chopped
$^3/_4$ of a 16 oz. box of Rotini pasta cooked as directed on
    box (boil 10 minutes) drain and rinse with cold water
$^1/_2$ medium onion - chopped
2 - 8 oz. bottles of no-fat Thousand Island Salad Dressing
    (by Hidden Valley Ranch)

Mix Thousand Island Salad Dressing with tuna, onion, cheese
and egg whites. Toss with cooled and drained pasta.

Chill. Great served chilled in $^1/_2$ of cantaloupe! Cut bottom of
melons off to make a bowl out of the cantaloupe.

Yield: 6 entree size servings   Calories: 348   Fat: 1.1 grams
    12 side dishes   Calories: 174   Fat: 0.6 grams

♥♥♥♥♥♥♥♥♥♥♥♥♥♥♥♥♥♥♥♥♥♥♥♥♥♥♥

♥ *Taco Salad* ♥

This is a very hearty, stick to your bones type salad! Eat as a meal or a side dish.

1 lb. ground eye of round (beef)
1 envelope of your favorite brand of taco seasoning mix
³/₄ cup water

Brown hamburger. Drain any juices. Add taco seasoning mix and water. Bring to a boil. Reduce heat. Simmer for 15 minutes. Remove from heat. Let cool.

2 large heads of Iceburg lettuce torn into bit size pieces
8 oz. fat-free shredded cheddar cheese
4 fresh tomatoes - diced
1 medium onion - chopped
8 oz. fat-free "Western" salad dressing (use more if desired)
48 (2 oz.) low-fat tortilla chips - crushed

In a very large bowl toss lettuce with fat-free cheddar cheese, diced tomatoes, chopped onion. (If desired you can use the seasoned taco meat warmed or cooled. I would encourage you NOT to put the meat in warm, unless you are going to eat the salad immediately.)

Toss the seasoned taco meat, tortilla chips, salad dressing and sour cream in salad right before serving. You don't want to put the last four ingredients in salad too soon before eating or lettuce will become wilted and tortilla chips will become soggy.

This is excellent served as a meal!

Yield:	6 main meals	Calories: 243	Fat: 3.16 grams
	12 side dishes	Calories: 122	Fat: 1.58 grams

IN ORDER TO SHINE, SOME OF US NEED MORE
POLISHING THAN OTHERS.

♥♥♥♥♥♥♥♥♥♥♥♥♥♥♥♥♥♥♥♥♥♥♥♥♥♥♥

♥♥♥♥♥♥♥♥♥♥♥♥♥♥♥♥♥♥♥♥♥♥♥♥♥♥

♥ *Seafood Chowder* ♥

*This is a special treat anytime! Use as an appetizer
or as a main meal! Excellent!!*

1 envelope Butter Buds - dry
$^1/_3$ cup carrot - shredded
1 - 14$^1/_2$ oz. can chicken broth
$^3/_4$ cup sliced mushrooms
1 Tbs. garlic salt (optional)
$^1/_2$ cup onion - chopped
1 - 10 oz. can baby clams - with juices
$^1/_2$ tsp. thyme (rub between palms of hands before putting
   in to make fine)
1 lb. shrimp - cleaned (if using medium or large size-cut in
   $^1/_2$'s lengthwise)
3 cups skim milk
4 Tbs. flour
8 oz. crab meat - cut into bite size pieces (imitation may be
   used)
dash of pepper - optional

In Dutch Oven or large sauce pan, put chicken broth, carrots,
Butter Buds, garlic salt, mushrooms, onions and thyme. Bring
to a boil. Reduce heat to a very low simmer. Add shrimp,
clams with its juices, and bite size pieces of crabmeat. Stir in 2
cups of milk. With the remaining one cup of milk stir in the 4
Tbs. of flour. Quickly stir the 1 cup of milk and flour until
flour is dissolved. Pour into chowder. Stir for about 5 minutes
until thick and creamy.

Serve hot.

Yield: 7 - 1 cup servings

Calories: 156
Fat: 1.43 grams

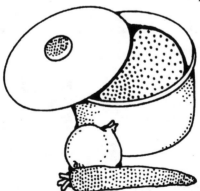

♥♥♥♥♥♥♥♥♥♥♥♥♥♥♥♥♥♥♥♥♥♥♥♥♥♥

♥ *Broccoli & Potato Casserole* ♥

If you like twice baked potatoes you'll like this!

8 medium potatoes (approx. 2 lbs.)
2 cups skim milk
¼ cup no-fat sour cream
4 oz. fat-free Ultra Promise Margarine
16 oz. bag of frozen broccoli
1 cup sour cream & onion Skinnys (or Frito Lay Baked Low
   Fat Potato Chips)
1 - 9 oz. pk. of Good Seasons Fat-Free Zesty Herb Salad
   Dressing Mix
1 pkg. Hidden Valley Ranch Reduced Calorie Salad
   Dressing Mix

What I'd encourage you to do if you're having baked potatoes,
make about 2 lbs. more (approx. 8 medium to small potatoes)
and keep in the refrigerator until ready to make this recipe.
Once the potatoes are cooled easily peel off the skins with
your fingers. Discard skins. Put peeled potatoes in large bowl.
Add both salad dressing packets, 2 cups skim milk and ¼ cup
no-fat sour cream to potatoes. Break potatoes up enough so
that the mixer will work smoothly. Beat on medium for about
1½ - 2 minutes. It will be creamy with some lumps in it. Set
aside. Cook broccoli in microwave as directed on package.
Drain water. With large spoon gently mix broccoli with potato
mixture.

Spray a 9" x 13" pan with non-fat cooking spray. Put potato-
broccoli mixture in pan and bake at 350 degrees for ½ hour.
Crush Skinnys to make 1 cup. Sprinkle over potato-broccoli
mixture and bake. Put back in oven for 1½-2 minutes at 450
degrees. Broil until top is toasty brown.

Serve warm.

Yield: 12 servings   Calories: 130   Fat: 0.3

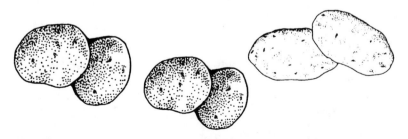

♥♥♥♥♥♥♥♥♥♥♥♥♥♥♥♥♥♥♥♥♥♥♥♥♥♥♥

♥ French Fries—The Healthy Ones ♥

My daughters love eating these fries! They compare restaurant fries to mine and 9 times out of 10 they say, "Those fries were okay, but not as good as your's, Mom!"

    non-fat cooking spray
    Lawry's seasoning salt
    4 Potatoes - Your favorite type of potato

- cut into long strips, 1/4" thickness
- spray cookie sheet with non-fat cooking spray
- lay potato (fries) on cookie sheet. Do not let edges touch each other!
- spray tops with non-fat cooking spray
- lightly sprinkle with Lawry's seasoning salt
- bake at 350 degrees for 20 minutes
- turn fries over
- spray with non-fat cooking spray
- bake another 15-20 minutes
- fries will be crispy and golden when done

* Note: The calories would be the same as eating a baked potato except for the few seconds of non-fat cooking spray you use. So use it sparingly!

Yield: 4 servings   Calories: 135   Fat: 2 grams

♥ Acorn Squash Bake ♥

    12 acorn squash
    1 cup dark brown sugar
    3/4 cup lite pancake syrup (maple flavor)
    8 oz. Ultra Fat-Free Promise
    1/2 tsp. lite salt

Cut acorn squash in 1/2 (clean seeds out), bake at 350 degrees for 45 minutes. Cool.

Scoop out meat of squash in large bowl. Add all ingredients. Beat on medium speed until well blended.

Keep refrigerated until ready to eat. Microwave for about 5-7 minutes or until warm.

Serve warm.

Yield: 24 servings (1/2 an acorn) Calories: 116 Fat: 0.2 grams
♥♥♥♥♥♥♥♥♥♥♥♥♥♥♥♥♥♥♥♥♥♥♥♥♥♥♥

Main Dishes & Casseroles

Mini Contents

(Main Dishes & Casseroles)

♥♥♥♥♥♥♥♥♥♥♥♥♥♥♥♥♥♥♥♥♥♥♥

♥ *Fried Chicken Strips* ♥

Great served plain or with your favorite fat-free salad dressing as a dip.

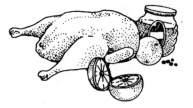

³/₄ cup toasted bread crumbs
¹/₄ cup whole wheat flour
2 tsp. garlic salt
¹/₄ tsp. ground black pepper
1 Tbs. grated Parmesan cheese

Mix together well. Set aside.

4 egg whites
¹/₃ cup skim milk
1 lb. boneless, skinless chicken breast - with all visible fat
cut off. Cut into ¹/₂" wide long strips.

Whip egg whites and milk together with whisk or beater for 1
minute. One at a time, dip cut chicken strips into egg mixture.
Let excess drain off chicken after it's been dipped. Now dip
into dry bread crumb mixture. Repeat this process again,
dipping each chicken strip into egg, then crumb mixture twice.

Place prepared chicken strips on cookie sheet that has been
sprayed with a non-fat cooking spray. Spray chicken strips
with no-fat cooking spray.

Bake at 400 degrees for 8-10 minutes. Turn over and bake an
additional 7-10 minutes. Bottoms will be golden brown when
ready to turn.

Yield: 6 servings   Calories: 129   Fat: 1.5 grams

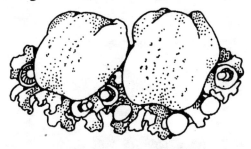

IT'S NOT FAIR THAT SOME PEOPLE ARE FAT AND
OTHERS EAT NON-STOP AND ARE NOT FAT. WHEN I GET
TO HEAVEN I'M TALKING TO GOD ABOUT THIS. I THINK
MEAN PEOPLE SHOULD BE FAT, AND SWEET, KIND,
WONDERFUL PEOPLE SHOULD BE THIN.

♥♥♥♥♥♥♥♥♥♥♥♥♥♥♥♥♥♥♥♥♥♥♥

♥♥♥♥♥♥♥♥♥♥♥♥♥♥♥♥♥♥♥♥♥♥♥♥♥♥♥

♥ *Teriyaki Chicken Kebobs* ♥

This dish is excellent served with my Seasoned Rice recipe!

Kebob Ingredients:
- 2 lbs boneless, skinless chicken breast - cut into 1" - 1½" chunks
- one whole fresh pineapple - cleaned and cut up into ½" - 1" chunks
- 3 - 4 medium size sweet onions - cut into ⅛'s
- 8 kebob stick skewers
- 2 fresh green peppers cut into ⅛'s
- 2 fresh red peppers cut into ⅛'s

Marinade sauce:
- 1 cup pineapple juice
- 1 cup lite teriyaki marinade sauce or lite soy sauce (either one, they are both made by LaChoy)
- ½ tsp. ground ginger
- ½ tsp. garlic powder

At least 2-3 hours before serving (or chicken can also be marinated a day or 2 in advance) marinate cut-up chicken pieces. Before baking in any fashion you desire, put chicken piece, onion, pineapple and peppers on skewers. Pour marinate over chicken kebob skewers and bake at 350 degrees for 15-20 minutes or until fully cooked.

After fully cooked, drain marinade into medium size sauce pan. Add 2-3 Tbs. cornstarch over medium-low heat, stirring constantly until smooth and creamy.

If desired, place cooked kebob on top of a bed of seasoned rice. Pour 2 Tbs. of marinade sauce over each kebob and rice. Serve remaining sauce in side dish for dipping chicken.

Yield: 8 servings   Calories: 301   Fat: 2.5 grams

♥♥♥♥♥♥♥♥♥♥♥♥♥♥♥♥♥♥♥♥♥♥♥♥♥♥♥

♥ *Oriental Teriyaki Beef Dinner* ♥

This meal is a huge hit with our children.

$^1/_2$ cup lite teriyaki marinade sauce (by LaChoy)
1 - 20 oz. can pineapple chunks in its own juice or $^1/_2$ cup
    pineapple juice
2 Tbs. cornstarch
$^1/_4$ tsp. ground ginger
$^1/_4$ tsp. garlic powder
1 medium to small onion cut into $^1/_8$'s (separate layers of
    onion)
1 lb. eye of round beef cut into $^1/_3$" bite size pieces (all
    visible fat removed)
4 cups frozen stir fry vegetables (oriental mixture with pea
    pods)

Drain juice from pineapple. Combine teriyaki marinade, pineapple juice, ground ginger and garlic powder in medium container. Mix well until ginger and garlic are completely dissolved. Add bite size pieces of beef and onion. Cover tightly and refrigerate, at least 15 minutes. (The longer this marinates the more flavorful the beef is. This can be done days in advance if desired)

Drain marinade and set aside. Use either a wok or a large pan. Spray pan with a non-fat cooking spray. Over medium heat cook meat and onions for about 5 minutes. Add frozen vegetables.

Add 2 Tbs. cornstarch to marinade and mix well until cornstarch is completely dissolved. Pour marinade over meat and vegetables being cooked. Stir and bring to a boil.

Cook for about 5 minutes until vegetables are slightly crisp yet tender. Serve with seasoned rice if desired. This dish is excellent served with my "Seasoned Rice" recipe.

Yield: 4 servings (not including rice)   Calories: 304
                                                         Fat: 6.75 grams

♥♥♥♥♥♥♥♥♥♥♥♥♥♥♥♥♥♥♥♥♥♥♥♥♥♥

♥ *3 in 1 Chicken Vegetable Soup* ♥

This is a hearty, down home, good eatin' country soup that's delicious...even in the suburbs and cities! These just aren't soups - they're a meal!

Once the main soup is made you have your choice; I like to make at least 1 other different kind of soup from the main base of this wonderful chicken vegetable soup. Follow these simple directions:

(Main Recipe)
Chicken Vegetable Soup:
  14 cups water
  4 chicken flavored bouillon cubes
  4 whole bay leaves
  1 - 15 to 16 oz. can of each:
    spinach
    asparagus
    sliced stewed tomatoes
    creamed corn
  1 - 16 oz. bag of frozen oriental style mixed vegetables
  1 - 16 oz. bag of frozen mixed vegetables
  1 tsp. sweet basil
  $1/2$ tsp. black pepper
  1 Tbs. garlic powder
  1 Tbs. garlic salt
  $2^1/_2$ - 3 cups chicken breast (approximately. 3 - 10 oz.
    chicken breasts)

Bring chicken to boil in 14 cups of water. (If not using boneless chicken breast boil for about 5 minutes. Remove chicken from water and debone if necessary). Remove fat from chicken water by pouring chicken water through a strainer filled with ice that is over a large pot. The ice will collect the fat from the water. If needed, do it 2 or 3 times. Add all ingredients to chicken water. Once again bring to a boil. If desired you can now make 2 of the 3 recipes from this main soup.

Yield: 29 servings 1 cup each   Calories: 89
                                        Fat: 1.4 grams

1. Chicken Vegetable Soup - It's all done now except the eatin'.

TOO MUCH OF ANYTHING
- NO MATTER HOW GOOD IT IS - IS TOO MUCH!

♥♥♥♥♥♥♥♥♥♥♥♥♥♥♥♥♥♥♥♥♥♥♥♥♥♥

<u>2. Chicken Noodle Vegetable Soup -</u> Take half of the recipe above, add 2 cups more water. Bring to a boil. Add 12 oz. bag of noodles. (For lower fat intake "No Yolks" noodles may be used if desired.) Stir vigorously until soup boils again. (Approximately 30 seconds.) Boil for 6-7 minutes. Serve hot.

Chicken Noodle Vegetable Soup - approximately 14 cups. 1 cup is 1.6 grams of fat and 185 calories.

<u>3. Chicken Rice Vegetable Soup -</u> Add 1 cup long grain rice to half of the main recipe - chicken vegetable soup. Bring to a boil, reduce heat, cover tightly and simmer for 20 minutes. Serve hot.

Chicken Rice Vegetable Soup - Approximately 12 cups. 1 cup is 1.5 grams of fat and 146 calories.

Very important!! Remove bay leaves before eating!

Note: As I said earlier, these are hearty soups. If you like brothier soup, simply add water or store-bought, canned chicken broth. I think Campbell's Ready to Serve Chicken Broth is good.

These soups can easily be reheated.

ONE OF THE GREATEST GIFTS WE CAN TEACH OUR CHILDREN IS TO BE RESPONSIBLE FOR THEIR ACTIONS.

♥♥♥♥♥♥♥♥♥♥♥♥♥♥♥♥♥♥♥♥♥♥♥♥♥♥♥

❤❤❤❤❤❤❤❤❤❤❤❤❤❤❤❤❤❤❤❤❤❤❤❤❤❤

❤ *2 Dinners in One Roast* ❤

This can serve 12 at 298 calories ('/₄ lb. beef each) or eat '/₂ of this recipe and save 2nd half for stew.

Meal #1 Pot Roast

3 lb. eye of round (beef) - all visible fat trimmed off
12 potatoes - cut into '/₈'s
8 medium onions - cup into '/₈'s
1 pkg. dry onion soup mix (approximately 1.37 oz.)
2 cups water
2 lbs. fresh carrots - peeled and cut into 3" - 4" lengths

In large Dutch Oven or roaster pan add water and dry soup mix until soup is dissolved. Put remaining ingredients, in this order on top of roast: potatoes, onions, carrots.

Bake at 375 degrees for 3 hours or put in crockpot on medium heat for 4-5 hours.
Eat '/₂ of this prepared meal. Save 2nd half.

Yield: 12 servings   Calories: 298   Fat: 5.8 grams

Meal #2 - Stew

Use '/₂ of prepared leftover juices and onion soup from first meal above and add:
  4 cups skim milk
  1 cup corn starch
  '/₈ tsp. ground black pepper
  '/₄ tsp. dried basil
  1 tsp. garlic salt
  1 tsp. A-1 Sauce
  1 - 16 oz. can sweet peas - drained
  1 tsp. lite salt
Chop leftover eye of round roast into small bite size pieces.

Drain onion soup from meal into 2 quart saucepan. Add 3 cups milk and warm on medium-low heat. In bowl add remaining 1 cup cold skim milk with 1 cup corn starch. Stir until corn starch is completely dissolved. Add milk - cornstarch mixture to milk-soup mixture. Add all seasonings and A-1 Sauce. Stir constantly until gravy is thick and creamy.

Pour gravy over potatoes, onions, cut-up roast and carrots. Add peas. Stir until completely covered with gravy. Cover and keep refrigerated for up to 5 days. Just heat before serving. If desired, the second meal can be frozen until ready to use.

Yield: 12 servings   Calories: 185   Fat: 3 grams

❤❤❤❤❤❤❤❤❤❤❤❤❤❤❤❤❤❤❤❤❤❤❤❤❤❤

♥ Sweet & Sassy Meatballs ♥

Easy! These are always a big hit! Serve as an appetizer or as an entree for a meal.

Meatballs:
- 1 lb. ground eye of round (beef)
- 1/2 cup bread crumbs
- 3 egg whites
- 1 small onion - finely chopped
- 1/4 tsp. lite salt
- 1/4 tsp. pepper

Beat egg whites with fork. Add all remaining ingredients and mix until well blended.

With a measuring utensil measure out 1 Tbs. of meat mixture. Roll into ball with hands. Repeat with rest of mixture. Makes approximately 25 meatballs.

Sauce:
- 1 - 8 oz. can tomato sauce
- 3/4 cup ketchup
- 1/4 cup firmly packed brown sugar (light or dark)
- 2 Tbs. Nutra-Sweet® Spoonful™ (OR 2 tbs. sugar)

Mix with fork until sauce is well blended.

For easier clean up, cover cookie sheet or jelly roll pan with foil. Spray with a non-fat cooking spray. Dip each meatball completely in sauce. Place meatballs on foil that has been sprayed with a no-fat cooking spray.

Bake at 350 degrees for 30 minutes. With tongs *dip each meatball (once again) completely into sauce. Place meatballs back onto foiled sheet and return to 350 degree oven for 15 minutes.

Serve immediately.
*For easier dipping of the meatballs, pour the sauce (once made) into a cup.

Appetizer - 25 servings (1 Tbs. size)
   With Nutra-Sweet® Spoonful™: Calories: 53   Fat: 1 gram
   With sugar: Calories: 57   Fat: 1 gram

Entree - 5 meatballs a serving
   With Nutra-Sweet® Spoonful™: Calories: 265 Fat: 5.2 grams
   With sugar: Calories: 283   Fat: 5.2 grams

❤❤❤❤❤❤❤❤❤❤❤❤❤❤❤❤❤❤❤❤❤❤❤❤❤❤

❤ *"Seconds Please" Meatloaf* ❤

³/₄ cup Italian seasoned bread crumbs
1 lb ground eye of round (beef)
14 oz. - 16 oz. Healthy Choice smoked sausage
1 medium onion - chopped
1 small green pepper - chopped
¹/₂ tsp. salt - optional
¹/₂ tsp. pepper
2 egg whites - beaten

Topping:
  ¹/₂ cup ketchup
  8 oz. tomato sauce
  ¹/₃ cup brown sugar
  8 packets of Equal® (OR ¹/₃ cup sugar)

Grind smoked sausage in food processor or blender. In large
bowl add all ingredients and mix well.

For easier cleanup cover a jelly roll pan (a cookie sheet with
edges) with foil. Spray with a non-fat cooking spray. With
hands shape meatloaf mixture into a loaf.

Bake at 350 degrees for 35-40 minutes.

While meatloaf is baking mix topping ingredients in medium
size bowl. Spoon mixture over meatloaf. Return meatloaf to
oven and bake an additional ¹/₂ hour.

Yield: 8 servings
              With Equal®: Calories: 187   Fat: 3.2 grams
              With sugar: Calories: 217   Fat: 3.2 grams

❤ *Creamy Macaroni and Cheese* ❤

16 oz. large pasta shells, boiled and drained
16 oz. fat-free sharp cheese - cut into small pieces
2 oz. fat-free shredded cheddar cheese
12 oz. can of lite evaporated skimmed milk
¹/₂ tsp. lite salt (optional)

Cook and drain pasta as directed on box. In same pan add
both cheeses and evaporated milk over low heat on stove. Add
salt. Serve warm immediately.

Yield: 8 servings   Calories: 318   Fat: 0.9 grams
❤❤❤❤❤❤❤❤❤❤❤❤❤❤❤❤❤❤❤❤❤❤❤❤

♥♥♥♥♥♥♥♥♥♥♥♥♥♥♥♥♥♥♥♥♥♥♥♥♥♥♥♥

♥ *Baked Vermicelli* ♥

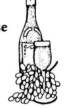

1 lb. ground eye of round (beef)
$^1/_2$ tsp. ground sage
1 - 30 oz. jar of your favorite spaghetti sauce (I use
    Healthy Choice)
20 oz. fat-free ricotta cheese
2 Tbs. grated Parmesan cheese
8 oz. fat-free mozzarella cheese
16 oz. vermicelli

In large pan brown beef with sage. Add spaghetti sauce to hamburger. Turn off heat.

Cook vermicelli as directed on package, drain water. Stir cooked vermicelli with spaghetti sauce.

Spray a 9" x 13" pan with a non-fat cooking spray. Pour vermicelli with sauce into pan. Spread ricotta cheese on top. Sprinkle with Parmesan then mozzarella cheese on top of Parmesan.

Bake at 350 degrees for 30 minutes.

This can be made in advance and either frozen or kept refrigerated until ready to use. (Up to 3 days refrigerated or up to four weeks in the freezer. Bake 15-20 minutes longer if taken directly from the freezer).

Yield: 12 servings   Calories: 270   Fat: 2.3 grams

♥ *Cheesie Tuna Casserole* ♥

16 oz. large pasta shells, boiled and drained for 13 minutes
16 oz. fat-free sharp cheese - cut into small pieces
2 oz. fat-free shredded cheddar cheese
12 oz. can of lite evaporated skimmed milk
$^1/_2$ tsp. lite salt (optional)
6 oz. can of tuna in water
4 oz. can of mushroom pieces

Cook and drain pasta as directed on box. In same pan add both cheeses and evaporated milk over low heat on stove. Add tuna, mushrooms and salt. Serve warm immediately.

Yield: 8 servings   Calories: 347   Fat: 1.1 grams

♥♥♥♥♥♥♥♥♥♥♥♥♥♥♥♥♥♥♥♥♥♥♥♥♥♥♥♥

♥♥♥♥♥♥♥♥♥♥♥♥♥♥♥♥♥♥♥♥♥♥♥♥♥♥♥♥

♥ *Thick Chili* ♥

4 lbs. ground eye of round (beef)
2 onions - chopped
$1/2$ tsp. chili powder
1 - 31 oz. can Brooks Chili Hot Beans in Chili Sauce
1 - 16 oz. can stewed tomatoes - sliced
3 - 16 oz. cans of tomato paste
1 - 8 oz. can of tomato sauce
2 Tbs. water
2 tsp. garlic

Brown beef in large pan. Drain and rinse beef in strainer to eliminate any fat.

Sauté chopped onion in 2 Tbs. water until soft. Add browned beef, chili powder and all remaining ingredients. Mix well.

Simmer 10-15 minutes. Serve warm.

Yield: 21 servings (8 oz. each)   Calories: 256   Fat: 5 grams

♥ *Chili Mac* ♥

4 lbs. ground eye of round (beef)
1 lb. cooked spaghetti or elbow macaroni
2 onions - chopped
$1/2$ tsp. chili powder
1 - 31 oz. can Brooks Chili Hot Beans in Chili Sauce
1 - 16 oz. can stewed tomatoes - sliced
3 - 6 oz. cans of tomato paste
1 - 8 oz. can of tomato sauce
2 Tbs. water
1 tsp. garlic

Brown beef in large pan. Drain and rinse beef, with cold water, in strainer to eliminate any fat.

Cook chopped onion in 2 Tbs. water until soft. Add browned beef, chili powder and all remaining ingredients. Mix well.

Simmer 10-15 minutes. Sprinkle with grated Italian topping (if desired).

Serve warm.

Yield: 23 servings (8 oz. each)   Calories: 307   Fat: 5 grams
♥♥♥♥♥♥♥♥♥♥♥♥♥♥♥♥♥♥♥♥♥♥♥♥♥♥♥♥

♥♥♥♥♥♥♥♥♥♥♥♥♥♥♥♥♥♥♥♥♥♥♥♥♥♥♥

♥ *Low-Fat Cheesie Taco Pie* ♥

4 Tbs. Molly McButter cheese sprinkles
14 oz. low-fat tortilla chips
3 to 4 Tbs. water
14 slices fat-free sharp cheddar cheese (I use "Borden")
1 - 15³/₄ oz. Brooks Chili Hot Beans in Chili Sauce
1 lb. ground eye of round (beef)
1 - 1¹/₄ oz. pkg. of taco seasoning mix (I use Ortega)
¹/₂ cup salsa
1 pint cherry tomatoes
2 cups shredded lettuce
¹/₃ cup no-fat sour cream (I use Land O'Lakes)
no-fat French salad dressing (I like Henri's)

With food processor crumble ¹/₂ of the bag of tortilla chips with 4 Tbs. of Molly McButter cheese sprinkles. Reserve ¹/₂ cup of crumbs for later. Add 3 Tbs. water and press remaining mixture into 9" pie pan that has been sprayed with a non-fat cooking spray to form the crust. Lay 4 slices of no-fat cheese on crust. Corners of cheese will show.

Combine 6 slices of no-fat cheese slices and a can of chili hot beans. Blend for 15-20 seconds. Pour ³/₄ of mixture on top of cheese slices, with spoon press onto the sides of the pie pan up the edges to the top. Reserve ¹/₄ of the mixture.

Brown beef. Drain. Add package of taco seasoning with ³/₄ cup water. Simmer 15 minutes on low heat. Pour taco meat over bean mixture. Lay 4 slices of no-fat cheese on top of taco meat. Sprinkle reserved crumb mixture previously made with chips over taco meat.

Bake at 350 degrees for 30 minutes. Put shredded lettuce on top of warm pie. Top with cherry tomatoes then no-fat sour cream and drizzle no-fat French salad dressing. Serve warm immediately.

With the remaining ¹/₄ of chili hot bean & cheese mixture (that was put aside) add ¹/₂ cup salsa. Warm in microwave for 1¹/₂ - 2 minutes. Serve as dip with the remaining bag of tortilla chips.

Yield: 8 servings   Calories: 389   Fat: 5.4

IF YOU WANT TO GIVE YOURSELF A DOSE OF GOOD
MEDICINE, DO SOMETHING FOR SOMEONE ELSE FOR NO
OTHER REASON THAN TO BLESS THEM.

♥♥♥♥♥♥♥♥♥♥♥♥♥♥♥♥♥♥♥♥♥♥♥♥♥♥♥

♥♥♥♥♥♥♥♥♥♥♥♥♥♥♥♥♥♥♥♥♥♥♥♥♥♥♥♥♥

♥ *Spinach Lasagna* ♥

1 lb. lasagna noodles (use spinach lasagna noodles if
  available) cooked
2 - 15 oz. fat-free ricotta cheese
4 egg whites
1 - 8 oz. fat-free sour cream
2 - 10 oz. pkgs. of frozen chopped spinach - thawed & well
  drained
1 lb. fat-free mozzarella cheese
2 - 26 oz. jars Healthy Choice spaghetti sauce with meat
¾ cup grated Italian topping (or grated parmesan cheese)
3 oz. finely shredded Parmesan cheese

Beat egg whites for 30 seconds, add ricotta cheese, sour
cream, parmesan cheese, grated Italian topping and the
spinach. Mix well on medium with mixer.

Spray a 9" x 13" and a 7" x 10" pan, each with a non-fat
cooking spray. Put a little spaghetti sauce in bottom of each
pan before layering lasagna noodles, cheese-spinach mixture,
spaghetti sauce and mozzarella cheese in that order. Keep
layering in that exact order until you reach the top of the pan.
End with spaghetti sauce and sprinkle with mozzarella cheese.

Total baking time is 1 hour. Bake at 375 degrees for 45
minutes then reduce heat to 350 degrees for an additional 15
minutes.

This recipe will make 2 pans. One 9" x 13" and one 7" x 10".

Let cool for 5 minutes before serving.

Yield: 14 servings   Calories: 360   Fat: 6 grams

STAY FOCUSED ON ALL THAT IS GOOD,
RIGHT AND TRUE.

♥♥♥♥♥♥♥♥♥♥♥♥♥♥♥♥♥♥♥♥♥♥♥♥♥♥♥♥♥

♥♥♥♥♥♥♥♥♥♥♥♥♥♥♥♥♥♥♥♥♥♥♥♥♥

♥ *Four Cheese Lasagna* ♥

1 - 16 oz. box of lasagna noodles (prepared as directed on box)
24 oz. fat-free cottage cheese
15 oz. fat-free ricotta cheese
1 lb. shredded fat-free mozzarella cheese
1 lb. shredded fat-free Healthy Choice Mexican cheese
4 egg whites
30 oz. jar Prego Three Cheese Spaghetti Sauce (if desired)

Beat egg whites with cottage cheese and ricotta cheese for 1 minute on high. Spray 9" x 13" pan with a non-fat cooking spray. Layer in this order:

Lasagna noodles
1$\frac{1}{3}$ cups ricotta & cottage cheese mixture
$\frac{1}{2}$ lb. Mexican cheese
lasagna noodles
1$\frac{1}{3}$ cups ricotta & cottage cheese mixture
$\frac{1}{3}$ lb. mozzarella cheese
lasagna noodles
1$\frac{1}{3}$ cups ricotta & cottage cheese mixture
$\frac{1}{3}$ lb. mozzarella cheese
lasagna noodles
$\frac{1}{3}$ lb. mozzarella cheese
$\frac{1}{2}$ lb. Mexican cheese

Bake at 350 degrees for 50 minutes.

Let cool for a couple of minutes before cutting.

In microwave warm spaghetti sauce. When serving take $\frac{1}{12}$ of the baked cheese lasagna and pour $\frac{1}{4}$ cup of spaghetti sauce on top - if desired.

Yield: 12 servings   Calories: 303   Fat: Less than 1 gram
with spaghetti sauce: Calories: 353   Fat: 2 grams

LORD, LET ME BE A LIVING EXAMPLE OF YOUR LOVE.

♥♥♥♥♥♥♥♥♥♥♥♥♥♥♥♥♥♥♥♥♥♥♥♥♥

❤ *Mexican Lasagna* ❤

If you like spicy foods you'll like this.
This meal can be made days in advance and refrigerated until needed.
Just bake for 40-45 minutes instead of 30 minutes.

1 lb. lasagna noodles
1 lb. ground eye of round (beef)
1 pkg. taco seasoning mix (1¼ oz. size)
15 oz. fat-free ricotta cheese (I use Frigo brand)
1 lb. Healthy Choice fat-free shredded cheddar cheese (I
    like to use the fancy shredded cheese)
28 oz. chunky salsa (use your favorite brand)
2 egg whites

Beat egg whites with ricotta cheese, set aside. Prepare lasagna noodles as directed on box. Brown hamburger, drain and then prepare taco seasoning mix with hamburger as directed on back of seasoning package. Spray 9" x 13" pan with non-fat cooking spray. In this order layer lasagna from the bottom up:
   lasagna noodles
   ⅓ of the ricotta cheese mixture, spread thinly over
      noodles
   all of the taco seasoned hamburger
   ⅓ of the cheddar cheese
   lasagna noodles
   ½ of what's left of the ricotta cheese mixture
      (approximately 5 oz.) (spread thinly over noodles)
   ½ jar chunky salsa
   ⅓ of the cheddar cheese
   lasagna noodles
   rest of the ricotta cheese mixture
   rest of chunky salsa
   rest of cheddar cheese

Bake at 350 degrees for ½ hour or until thoroughly warmed.

Yield: 12 servings   Calories: 290   Fat: 2 grams

❤❤❤❤❤❤❤❤❤❤❤❤❤❤❤❤❤❤❤❤❤❤❤❤❤

❤ *Vegetable Lasagna* ❤

6 cups frozen vegetables - your favorite blend (I like
   broccoli, carrots, mushrooms and onions)
20 oz. of fat-free ricotta cheese
1 cup fat-free cottage cheese
4 egg whites
8 oz. fat-free shredded mozzarella cheese (I use Healthy
   Choice)
8 oz. fat-free shredded cheddar cheese (I use Healthy
   Choice)
1 packet of Butter Buds (¹/₂ oz.) - dry
1 tsp. garlic salt or garlic powder - whichever you prefer
16 oz. lasagna noodles - prepared as directed on box
26 oz. jar of your favorite fat-free spaghetti sauce
   (optional)

Beat ricotta cheese, cottage cheese, egg whites, Butter Buds
and garlic salt until well blended. Divide cheese mixture into 3
bowls, putting ¹/₃ of the cheese mixture into each bowl. Add 2
cups of the frozen vegetables into <u>each</u> bowl along with the
cheese mixture.

In one bowl, with cheese mixture, add 4 oz. of shredded
cheddar cheese, mix well. In another bowl with cheese
mixture add 4 oz. of shredded mozzarella cheese, mix well.

Spray a 9" x 13" pan with a non-fat cooking spray. In this
exact order layer from the bottom of the pan up: lasagna
noodles, mozzarella vegetable cheese mixture, lasagna,
cheddar vegetable cheese mixture, lasagna, vegetable cheese
mixtures. With remaining mozzarella shredded and cheddar
shredded cheese (approximately 4 oz. each) sprinkle cheeses
together over lasagna and press into vegetable cheese mixture.
Bake at 350 degrees for 30 minutes.

Some lasagna noodles may be left over. This can be made in
advance and refrigerated until ready to bake. If desired,
microwave your favorite spaghetti sauce and spoon over each
serving.

Yield: 12 servings   Calories: 265   Fat: .66 grams

❤❤❤❤❤❤❤❤❤❤❤❤❤❤❤❤❤❤❤❤❤❤❤❤❤

♥♥♥♥♥♥♥♥♥♥♥♥♥♥♥♥♥♥♥♥♥♥♥♥♥♥♥

♥ *Lasagna Supreme* ♥
A huge hit for any special occasion meal!

¾ lb. fat-free mozzarella cheese (I use Healthy Choice)
6 Tbs. grated Parmesan cheese
15 oz. fat-free ricotta cheese (I use Frigo)
1 lb. lasagna - prepared as directed on package
27.5 oz. jar - Ragu Today's Chunky Garden Harvest
    Spaghetti Sauce
½ medium onion - chopped (approximately ¾ cup)
8 oz. fresh mushrooms - thinly sliced
1 lb. ground eye of round
14 oz. Healthy Choice Low-Fat Smoked Sausage
2 egg whites

Beat egg whites with ricotta cheese. Set aside. Grind up
sausage in food processor. Spray large saucepan with non-fat
cooking spray. Cook hamburger and sausage together until
fully cooked. Do not drain!! Add mushrooms and onion.
Cover and cook on low for 4 - 5 minutes. Add spaghetti sauce.
Mix well. Turn off heat and prepare to put lasagna together.

Spray a 9" x 13" pan with a non-fat cooking spray. Using 4
long lasagna noodles, cover the bottom of the pan. The sides
of the lasagna noodles will overlap slightly. In this exact order
from the <u>bottom</u> going up layer the lasagna:
    1½ cups meat sauce
    lasagna noodles
    1 cup ricotta cheese mixture
    1 cup mozzarella cheese
    sprinkle 2 Tbs. Parmesan cheese
    lasagna noodles
    1½ cup meat sauce
    lasagna noodles
    1 cup ricotta cheese mixture
    1 cup mozzarella cheese
    2 Tbs. Parmesan cheese
    lasagna noodles
    2 cups meat sauce
    1 cup mozzarella cheese
    2 Tbs. Parmesan cheese
Note: There will be a little extra sauce left over.

Bake at 350 degrees for 30 minutes. Let sit a few minutes
before cutting. (If you prepared this ahead of time and froze it,
bake for 45-55 minutes or until it is fully cooked.)

♥♥♥♥♥♥♥♥♥♥♥♥♥♥♥♥♥♥♥♥♥♥♥♥♥♥♥

I like making this ahead of time and either freezing it or putting it in the refrigerator until ready to use.

Yield: 12 Servings   Calories: 343   Fat: 4.6 grams

♥ *Steak on a Stick* ♥
Substitute chicken for the steak and have chicken sticks.

21 oz. can crushed pineapple in its own juices
2 lbs. eye of round steak
garlic salt - optional
kebob sticks

Cut steak into 1^1/$_2$" pieces, removing all visible fat. In Zip-loc gallon size bags marinate steak pieces in crushed pineapple, and juice, at least 8 hours. (The longer it is marinated the better I think it tastes.)

Arrange about 6 pieces of steak on kebob stick. Sprinkle lightly with garlic salt.

Cook on grill until desired doneness, turning once.

Yield: 8 servings   Calories: 191   Fat: 5.4 grams

♥ *Breakfast Bake* ♥

8 oz. of Healthy Choice Smoked Sausage - sliced thin
5 slices Fat-Free Borden Swiss Cheese - cubed
^{1}/$_2$ cup skim milk
7 egg whites
3 Tbs. fresh parsley (optional)
4 slices fat-free bread cubed
yellow food coloring

Beat 2 drops of yellow food coloring and egg whites. Combine all ingredients. Pour into a 9" x 13" pan that's been sprayed with a non-fat cooking spray.

Bake at 325 degrees for 30-35 minutes.

Yield: 8 servings   Calories: 95   Fat: 1.8 grams

♥♥♥♥♥♥♥♥♥♥♥♥♥♥♥♥♥♥♥♥♥♥♥♥♥♥

♥♥♥♥♥♥♥♥♥♥♥♥♥♥♥♥♥♥♥♥♥♥♥♥♥♥♥

♥ *Seafood Lasagna* ♥

Definitely an extra special meal for any special occasion!!

Seafood Sauce:
- 1 - 14½ oz. can clear chicken broth
- 2 - 10 oz. cans whole baby clams
- 1 packet Butter Buds - dry
- ½ cup onion - finely chopped
- 2 tsp. garlic salt
- 1 tsp. thyme (crush between your hands before adding dash of pepper)
- dash of pepper
- 8 oz. fully cooked crab meat (imitation may be used) - cut into bite size pieces
- 1 lb. fully cooked shrimp - cleaned and deveined (if shrimp are medium or large, cut in ½'s lengthwise)
- 1 cup cold non-fat buttermilk
- 1 Tbs. cornstarch

Mix cornstarch with buttermilk until completely dissolved. Over medium-low heat put all ingredients in large Dutch Oven. Bring to a boil, stirring often. Remove from heat. With a cup or ladle drain 1½ cup juices from the sauce and reserve for later.

- 16 oz. box of lasagna noodles - uncooked
- 20 oz. fat-free ricotta cheese
- 2 egg whites
- 8 oz. fat-free fancy mozzarella cheese - shredded
- ¼ cup bread crumbs - your favorite store bought brand is fine
- 3 Tbs. grated Parmesan cheese

Beat egg whites with ricotta cheese until well blended (about 1 minute); set aside. Spray a 9" x 13" pan with a non-fat cooking spray. Lay 5 strips of uncooked lasagna over seafood. Spread 1⅓ cup ricotta cheese mixture over pasta. Sprinkle with 4 oz. of mozzarella cheese. Then sprinkle with ½ Tbs. grated Parmesan cheese.

Lay 5 strips of uncooked lasagna noodles over cheese. Top with 2 cups seafood sauce. Lay 5 strips of uncooked lasagna over seafood. Spread remaining ricotta cheese mixture over lasagna. Spoon remaining seafood sauce over lasagna. Top with remaining mozzarella. Sprinkle with 2½ Tbs. of grated Parmesan cheese.

♥♥♥♥♥♥♥♥♥♥♥♥♥♥♥♥♥♥♥♥♥♥♥♥♥♥♥

Bake at 325 degrees for 1 hour.

Yield: 12 servings   Calories: 167   Fat: 1.25 grams

❤ *Spaghetti Pizza* ❤

> 4 egg whites
> $^1/_2$ cup skim milk
> 1 cup fat-free mozzarella cheese - shredded
> $^3/_4$ tsp. garlic powder
> 1 lb. spaghetti - cooked
> $^1/_2$ tsp. lite salt - optional

Topping:
> 32 oz. jar of low-fat spaghetti sauce (I like either Healthy
>   Choice or Ragu's lite brand)
> $^1/_2$ tsp. oregano
> 3 cups fat-free mozzarella cheese - shredded
> 3 cups of your favorite pizza toppings (chopped onions,
>   green peppers, mushrooms, etc.)

Combine egg whites, skim milk, 1 cup fat-free shredded mozzarella cheese, garlic powder and salt. Mix well. Add spaghetti. Spray a greased jelly roll pan (10" x 15" cookie sheet with edges) with a non-fat cooking spray. Put spaghetti mixture in pan. Bake at 350 degrees for 15 minutes.

Topping: Combine spaghetti sauce and oregano. Spread onto baked spaghetti. Sprinkle on 3 cups of the mozzarella cheese and arrange your favorite pizza toppings on top of cheese. Bake 30 minutes. Let sit 5 minutes before cutting. Makes 10 - 3" x 5" pieces.

Yield: 10 servings   Calories: 330   Fat: 1.0 grams

GOING TO CHURCH CAN HELP GET YOUR SPIRITUAL BATTERIES CHARGED.

❤❤❤❤❤❤❤❤❤❤❤❤❤❤❤❤❤❤❤❤❤❤❤❤❤❤

❤❤❤❤❤❤❤❤❤❤❤❤❤❤❤❤❤❤❤❤❤❤❤❤❤

❤ *Broccoli, Ham and Cheese Quiche* ❤

Makes 1 - 9" pie pan & 1 - 8" cheesecake spring form. Total 2 quiches

Crust:
> $^1/_2$ cup + 2 Tbs. no-fat cream cheese
> 1 cup buttermilk pancake mix

Mix dry pancake mix with no-fat cream cheese, on low.
Mixture will be dry and crumbly.

Spray pans with non-fat cooking spray. Spray hand with non-fat cooking spray. With sprayed hand divide mixture. Put $^2/_3$ of mixture in sprayed pie pan. With hand gently but firmly press dough up the sides of the pie pan to make a crust. Do bottom of pan last. Press with ball of hand to make sure that there are no cracks. Do the same to the cheesecake spring form, but do not go up the sides. If you don't have pie pans, use two 8" or 9" cake pans following the same procedure, but do not go up sides.

Bake crust for 7 minutes at 350 degrees.

Mixture:
> 3 drops of yellow food coloring
> 12 egg whites
> 1 cup fat-free ricotta cheese
> $^1/_2$ cup finely chopped onion (approx. 1 small onion)
> 6 oz. deli thin sliced ham (I use Healthy Choice)
> 1 - 4 oz. can sliced mushrooms - drained
> 2 cups cooked broccoli (If using frozen broccoli, pop it in
> the microwave and drain it after it is cooked.)
> 1 - 8 oz. pk. of fat-free shredded cheddar cheese (I use
> Healthy Choice)

Beat eggs, food coloring and ricotta cheese together on medium for 2 minutes. By hand, stir in remaining ingredients. Pour into prepared crust. If using a pie pan, cover sides of crust with foil. Bake at 350 degrees for 30-35 minutes. Remove foil if using pie pan the last 5 minutes. Serve warm. Great reheated in microwave.

Yield: 12 servings   Calories: 161   Fat: 1.16 grams

❤❤❤❤❤❤❤❤❤❤❤❤❤❤❤❤❤❤❤❤❤❤❤❤❤

♥♥♥♥♥♥♥♥♥♥♥♥♥♥♥♥♥♥♥♥♥♥♥♥♥♥♥♥

♥ Carol Strabley's Breakfast Souffle ♥

8 oz. Canadian Bacon
6 egg whites
5 slices of no-fat bread
1 cup no-fat cheddar cheese
2 cups skim milk
1 tsp. dry mustard
salt and pepper to taste

Mix all ingredients - put in a 9" x 9" dish sprayed with a non-fat cooking spray. Set overnight.

Bake at 350 degrees for 1 hour or until set.

Yield: 8 servings   Calories: 147   Fat: 2 grams

♥ Audrey's "Out of this World" Chicken Tenders ♥

1 - 2 lbs. chicken strips
¹/₂ of a fresh lemon
lemon & black pepper seasoning
seasoning salt
fat-free Italian dressing

Sprinkle fresh lemon juice, lemon & black pepper seasoning and seasoning salt on chicken strips. Marinate in Italian dressing for 1 - 2 days.

Spray pan with a no-fat cooking spray. Bake at 325 degrees for 30-45 minutes, turning over once. While still hot, put in a bowl with a lid, add 2 - 3 Tbs. of Italian dressing and shake.

Then eat and enjoy!!

Yield: Using 2 lbs. of chicken breast there are 8 servings - ¹/₄ lb. each   Calories: 200   Fat: 4 grams

♥♥♥♥♥♥♥♥♥♥♥♥♥♥♥♥♥♥♥♥♥♥♥♥♥♥♥♥

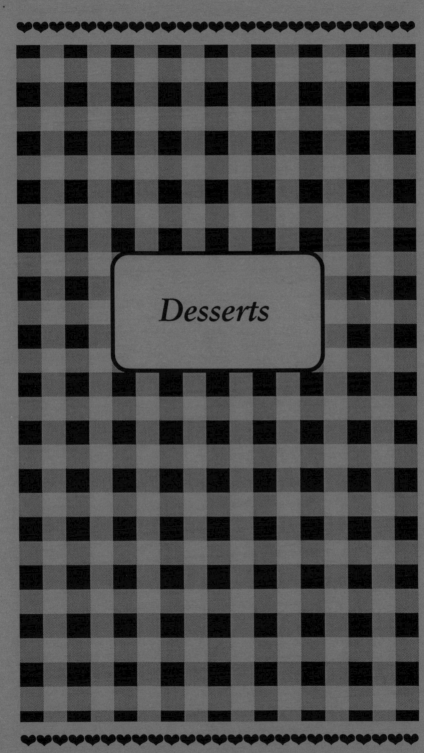

Desserts

Mini Contents

(Desserts)

♥♥♥♥♥♥♥♥♥♥♥♥♥♥♥♥♥♥♥♥♥♥♥♥♥

♥ *Sweet Cheese Dessert* ♥
Not a cheese cake, but resembles one.

1 tsp. vanilla
1 tsp. almond extract
5 egg whites
1 whole egg
4 Tbs. flour (I use 2 whole wheat and 2 all purpose)
2 - 8 oz. fat-free cream cheese (I use Health Valley)
1 - 24 oz. no-fat cottage cheese
²/₃ cup sugar } (OR 1 cup sugar)
¹/₃ cup Nutra Sweet® Spoonful™

Crust:
1 cup dry pancake mix (I use a brand with 2 grams fat per serving. There are many to choose from).

Beat cottage cheese 2-3 minutes until smooth and creamy. There may be some lumps; that's OK. Add in remaining ingredients except pancake mix. Beat for 2 minutes until well blended. Set aside.

In a separate bowl mix the 1 cup dry pancake mix with ¹/₃ cup of the cheese mixture you just made.

Spray a 9" x 13" pan with non-fat cooking spray.

Press crust mixture gently onto the bottom of the pan. (Do not do sides of pan.)

Pour cheese mixture over crust. Bake at 325 degrees for 1 hour or until center is set and top is lightly browned.

Let cool to room temperature, then refrigerate several hours until chilled thoroughly.

If desired spread 21 oz. can of either blueberry or cherry pie filling on top before refrigerating.

Yield: 15 servings
With sugar and Nutra Sweet® Spoonful™: Calories: 115
Fat: 0.4 grams
With sugar only: Calories: 131   Fat: 0.4 grams

THERE ARE SOME THINGS YOU SHOULDN'T PICK IN
PUBLIC: YOUR NOSE, YOUR SEAT OR ON OTHERS.

♥♥♥♥♥♥♥♥♥♥♥♥♥♥♥♥♥♥♥♥♥♥♥♥♥

❤❤❤❤❤❤❤❤❤❤❤❤❤❤❤❤❤❤❤❤❤❤❤❤

❤ *Strawberry Banana Trifle* ❤

This needs to be eaten within a day or it gets soggy.

3 bananas - sliced
4 - 4 serving size sugar-free pudding mix (I use "D Zerta")
8 medium-large sized fresh strawberries - sliced
2 packets Equal® (OR 4 tsp. sugar)
96 fat-free strawberry wafers (I use Sunshine brand)
6 cups skim milk

Toss strawberry slices with Equal and set aside.

Prepare pudding, using only 6 cups skim milk, as directed on package. Once boiling, remove from heat. Let cool 5 minutes, stirring twice.

Lay 48 wafers on bottom of a 9" x 13" or a 10" x 14" pan. Arrange bananas on wafers. Spread ½ of the pudding on top of bananas. Arrange 48 wafers on top of pudding. Arrange sweetened strawberry slices on top of wafer. Spread remaining pudding over sliced strawberries. Wrap with film and refrigerate at least 1 hour before serving.

Yield: 15 servings   With Equal®: Calories: 169   Fat: 0 grams
                       With sugar: Calories: 173   Fat: 0 grams

❤ *"Far Out" Fruity Fun Dessert* ❤

If you're really in a rush, use 2 store bought graham cracker crusts.

3 large bananas - sliced into ¼" pieces
1 - 20 oz. can lite cherry pie filling
1 - 20 oz. can crushed pineapple in its own juices
2 - 0.3 oz. boxes of sugar free strawberry Jello
6 Tbs. Fat-Free Ultra Promise Margarine
10 graham crackers crushed (each cracker has 4 segments)
¼ cup Nutra Sweet® Spoonful™ (OR ¼ cup sugar)

Melt fat-free margarine in microwave. Stir into crushed graham crackers and Nutra-Sweet. Mix until well blended.

Spray 9" x 13" pan with a non-fat cooking spray. Press crumb mixture in bottom pan. Set aside.

In a 2 quart saucepan bring cherry pie filling, crushed pineapple with its juices and 1 box of Jello to a boil. Boil for 1

❤❤❤❤❤❤❤❤❤❤❤❤❤❤❤❤❤❤❤❤❤❤❤❤

minute stirring constantly. Remove from heat. Add bananas. Pour over graham crackers.

Let cool in refrigerator for 1 hour. (*If using store bought crust, this will make 2 pies.)

Yield: 12 servings
With Nutra Sweet® Spoonful™: Calories: 149   Fat: 1.67 grams
With sugar: Calories: 169   Fat: 1.67 grams

♥ *Pumpkin Crunch Dessert* ♥
This recipe is a mix between a pie and a cake.

1 box Betty Crocker Super Moist Lite White Cake mix
1 - 29 oz. can of pumpkin
2 tsp. allspice
2 tsp. cinnamon
$^1/_2$ cup brown sugar

Mix well above ingredients with blender. Pour into a 9" x 13" pan that has been sprayed with a non-fat cooking spray.

Excellent Crumb Topping:
   $^3/_4$ cup brown sugar
   $^1/_2$ cup quick cooking oats
   $^3/_4$ cup whole wheat flour
   $1^1/_2$ tsp. cinnamon
   3 Tbs. Ultra Promise Fat-Free melted margarine

Mix all above ingredients with fork until crumbly. Sprinkle onto cake batter already in pan.

Bake at 350 degrees for 55-60 minutes.

Glaze:
   $^1/_4$ cup powdered sugar
   2 tsp. skim milk
   $^1/_2$ tsp. vanilla

Drizzle glaze over crumb topping while cake is still warm. Glaze will be thick but once drizzled on the cake, it will thin out.

Yield: 15 servings   Calories: 200   Fat: 2.1 grams

♥♥♥♥♥♥♥♥♥♥♥♥♥♥♥♥♥♥♥♥♥♥♥♥♥

♥♥♥♥♥♥♥♥♥♥♥♥♥♥♥♥♥♥♥♥♥♥♥♥♥♥

♥ Chocolate Raspberry OOO-La-La Dessert ♥

This is so elegant and so easy that it's hard to believe a dessert as special, tasty and elegant as this can be so easy! A definite hit for a special candlelight dinner!

1 store bought pound cake (approximately 12 oz.)
8 tsp. raspberry preserves
8 Tbs. Lite Cool Whip
8 Tbs. sugar-free, fat-free chocolate pudding (if using a box mix, prepare as directed on box) I used "D-Zerta" brand. There will be extra pudding left over. For super easy use, try Hershey's Fat-Free Pudding in the dairy section.

Cut pound cake in half as if making into a two layer cake. With a 2" cookie cutter (or biscuit cutter) cut out 8 round pieces from the cake (discard the crumbs) and put each into its own wide mouth (approximately 3" across opening) wine glass or pretty dessert cup. Spread 1 tsp. raspberry preserves on each little cake. Pour 1 Tbs. chocolate pudding on top of preserves. Top with one tablespoon Lite Cool Whip.

Presto! You are done!! (Is this easy or what?!)

This dessert can be made days ahead of time. Keep refrigerated until ready to serve. Insert toothpick in middle of each and cover with plastic wrap to keep each dessert creamy and fresh.

Yield: 8 servings   Calories: 174   Fat: 1 gram or less

IF IN THE FUTURE YOU WANT TO HAVE HAPPY MEMORIES - MAKE THEM NOW.

♥♥♥♥♥♥♥♥♥♥♥♥♥♥♥♥♥♥♥♥♥♥♥♥♥♥

♥♥♥♥♥♥♥♥♥♥♥♥♥♥♥♥♥♥♥♥♥♥♥♥♥♥♥

♥ *Tropical Baked Rice Dessert* ♥

This is an excellent dessert for someone who has ulcers. I like to make extra rice when preparing an oriental dish so that I have the rice ready to use when preparing this dessert.

10 egg whites
$^1/_2$ Tbs. coconut extract
$^1/_2$ cup brown sugar + $^1/_4$ cup brown sugar
$^1/_2$ cup skim milk
2 medium bananas - sliced
4 cups cooked long grain enriched rice

Beat egg whites with blender on high until foamy. Add coconut extract, brown sugar and skim milk. Beat until well blended. Add rice and beat until well blended. With spoon stir in bananas.

Spray a 9" x 13" pan with a non-fat cooking spray. Pour mixture into prepared pan and bake at 350 degrees for 30 minutes. With fingers, while still hot, sprinkle and smooth the remaining $^1/_4$ cup brown sugar on top.

Great served warm or chilled. I prefer it warm.

Yield: 15 servings   Calories: 124   Fat: 0 grams

LET ALL THAT YOU SAY AND DO REPRESENT THE
PERSON THAT YOU ARE.

REMEMBER, OUR ACTIONS SPEAK LOUDER THAN OUR
WORDS.

♥♥♥♥♥♥♥♥♥♥♥♥♥♥♥♥♥♥♥♥♥♥♥♥♥♥♥

❤❤❤❤❤❤❤❤❤❤❤❤❤❤❤❤❤❤❤❤❤❤❤❤❤❤

❤ Peach Crunch ❤

1¼ cups quick-cooking rolled oats
¾ cup brown sugar packed
½ cup whole wheat flour
2 tsp. ground cinnamon
9 medium sized fresh peaches
1 Tbs. sugar mixed with ½ tsp. cinnamon
½ cup Ultra Fat-Free Promise Margarine
a dash of lite salt (optional)

Slice peaches keeping skins on. Lightly toss peaches with sugar and cinnamon mixture. Put into 9" x 13" baking pan. Combine oats, flour, brown sugar, cinnamon and salt. Cut margarine into mixture with fork. Place lumpy dough over peaches as evenly as possible. (You will have some peaches here and there showing through).

Bake at 350 degrees for 45-50 minutes.

Great served warm with Dream Whip or no-fat vanilla yogurt.

Yield: 12 servings   Calories: 102   Fat: 0.5 grams

❤ So Good! So Delicious! So Easy! Jelly Roll Cake ❤

1 pkg. (18.5 oz.) Lovin' Lites yellow cake mix
1⅓ cup water
6 egg whites (or ¾ cup Egg Beaters)
20 oz. fruit preserves (Use your favorite flavor. They're all delicious.)

Make cake as directed on package. *Spray two jelly roll pans with no-fat spray. Pour ½ cup of cake batter into each pan and spread. Bake at 350 degrees for 10 minutes. Let cool. Spread each cake with about 7 oz. of preserves.

Roll each cake starting from the narrow side all the way until side view of finished rolled cake looks like this:
Spread remaining preserves (about 3 oz. each cake) on top.
Sprinkle with powdered sugar.

*A jelly roll pan is a cookie sheet with ½" edges.

Yield: 24 servings   Calories: 145   Fat: 2.1 grams
❤❤❤❤❤❤❤❤❤❤❤❤❤❤❤❤❤❤❤❤❤❤❤❤❤❤

❤❤❤❤❤❤❤❤❤❤❤❤❤❤❤❤❤❤❤❤❤❤❤❤❤❤❤❤

❤ *Strawberry Cream Crunch Fantasy* ❤

2 Tbs. dark brown sugar
2 cups crushed pretzels
1 pkg. Butter Buds - dry
3 Tbs. water

Mix above together well. Press into 8" cheese cake pan.

Bake 350 degrees for 10 minutes.

12 oz. fat-free cream cheese (I use Kraft Free)
12 packets Equal® (OR ½ cup sugar)
1 pkg. Dream Whip

Blend with mixer on high speed until blended. Spread on cooled pretzel crust above.

1 cup boiling water
1 pkg. sugar-free strawberry Jello (4 serving size)
1 cup sliced strawberries
4 packets Equal® (OR 3 tbs. plus 1 tsp. sugar)

Slice strawberries and sprinkle with the 4 packets of Equal. Set aside.

Stir sugar-free Jello into 1 cup boiling water. Add strawberries that have been sprinkled with Nutra-Sweet.

Chill. Once soft set, pour over cream cheese mixture.

Keep complete dessert chilled until ready to serve.

Yield: 6 servings   With Equal®: Calories: 102   Fat: 0.2
                          With sugar: Calories: 194   Fat: 0.2

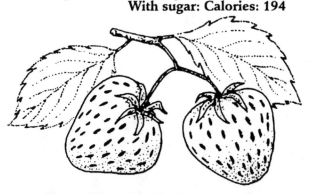

❤❤❤❤❤❤❤❤❤❤❤❤❤❤❤❤❤❤❤❤❤❤❤❤❤❤❤❤

♥♥♥♥♥♥♥♥♥♥♥♥♥♥♥♥♥♥♥♥♥♥♥♥♥♥♥♥

♥ *Harvest Pudding* ♥

16 egg whites
2¹/₃ cups skim milk
12 oz. can of lite evaporated skim milk
¹/₃ cup Nutra-Sweet® Spoonful™ (<u>OR</u> ¹/₃ c. sugar)
¹/₃ cup brown sugar - packed
1 tsp. vanilla
¹/₂ tsp. lite salt
¹/₂ tsp. cinnamon
¹/₂ tsp. ground cloves
8 slices lite (40 calorie) fat-free wheat bread - dried (best if
    laid out the night before to dry)
¹/₂ cup raisins
1 medium apple chopped thinly with skin on
    (approximately ³/₄ cup)

Beat together egg whites, milk, Nutra-Sweet, evaporated milk,
brown sugar, vanilla, lite salt, cinnamon and ground cloves,
until well mixed.

Spray a 9" x 13" pan with a non-fat cooking spray. Mix bread,
raisins and apples into egg mixture. Pour into prepared pan.

Bake at 325 degrees for 40-45 minutes or until a knife inserted
near the center comes out clean.

Serve warm with spicy creme topping.

Spicy Creme Topping:
    1 pkg. Dream Whip
    ¹/₂ cup cold milk
    ¹/₂ tsp. cinnamon
    ¹/₂ tsp. ground cloves

Yield: 12 servings
    With Nutra-Sweet® Spoonful™: Calories: 129   Fat: 0.2 grams
    With sugar: Calories: 150   Fat: 0.2 grams

THE BIBLE TELLS US THAT IT'S DURING THE HARD TIMES
THAT WE GROW. SOMETIMES I TELL GOD, "OK. GOD!
I'VE GROWN ENOUGH! THE HARD TIMES CAN STOP
NOW!"

♥♥♥♥♥♥♥♥♥♥♥♥♥♥♥♥♥♥♥♥♥♥♥♥♥♥♥♥

♥♥♥♥♥♥♥♥♥♥♥♥♥♥♥♥♥♥♥♥♥♥♥♥♥♥♥

♥ *Rhubarb Pudding* (easy) ♥

A tasty twist of Bread Pudding!
I got this recipe idea from one my Grandma Schaefer had, dated 1906.

2$\frac{1}{2}$ cups fresh rhubarb - diced thinly
1$\frac{1}{2}$ cups brown sugar - packed
5 slices fat-free bread cubed (I use Aunt Millies)
5 egg whites
2 cups skim milk
1 envelope Butter Buds - dry (do not add water!)

Spray a 9" x 13" pan with non-fat cooking spray. Arrange cubed bread and diced rhubarb in the 9" x 13" prepared pan. Set aside.

In a bowl beat egg whites until foamy - about 1 minute. Add milk and brown sugar. Beat on medium speed 1 minute more. Pour this mixture over bread and rhubarb in pan. With fork make sure mixture saturates all of the bread and rhubarb.

Sprinkle top with one envelope of Butter Buds.

Bake at 350 degrees for 1 hour.

Serve warm or cold. If served warm, I like to dab a little Lite Cool Whip on it.

Yield: 15 servings   Calories: 121   Fat: 0 grams

PUT YOUR LOVE INTO ACTION.

♥♥♥♥♥♥♥♥♥♥♥♥♥♥♥♥♥♥♥♥♥♥♥♥♥♥♥

♥♥♥♥♥♥♥♥♥♥♥♥♥♥♥♥♥♥♥♥♥♥♥♥♥♥

♥ Harvest Custard with an Autumn Topping ♥

I like to serve this warm, but it's also good chilled.
Refrigerate unused portions.

6 cups apples - thinly sliced and peeled
$^1/_2$ cup dark brown sugar
$^3/_4$ tsp. cinnamon
dash of ground cloves
8 egg whites
16 oz. fat-free sour cream
1 tsp. almond extract

Beat egg whites with fat-free sour cream. Add seasonings and brown sugar. Mix with blender until well blended. Stir in apples until apples are well coated.

Spray a 9" x 13" glass casserole dish with a non-fat cooking spray. Spread apple mixture evenly into pan. Set aside.

Topping:
  1 cup quick cooking rolled oats
  1 cup dark brown sugar
  $^1/_4$ cup all-purpose flour
  1 tsp. cinnamon
  dash of ground cloves
  $^1/_2$ cup Ultra Fat-Free Promise Margarine

Cut in margarine with oats, brown sugar, flour, cinnamon and ground cloves until mixture is well blended. With 2 forks take little bits of topping and evenly dot top of apple mixture with topping. (Use one fork to push off topping mixture off the other fork.)

Set casserole dish in pan of 1" water. (I used my broiling pan. My casserole dish sits perfectly in it. Try yours). Bake at 325 degrees for 50 minutes, or until knife inserted in middle comes out clean. Let set 5 minutes before cutting.

Yield: 15 servings   Calories: 102   Fat: 0.4 grams

SINCE WE CAN'T HAVE THE BEST OF EVERYTHING,
IT'S IMPORTANT TO MAKE THE BEST
OF EVERYTHING WE HAVE.

♥♥♥♥♥♥♥♥♥♥♥♥♥♥♥♥♥♥♥♥♥♥♥♥♥♥

♥ Applesauce Spice Squares ♥

Very good served warm and easy to make.

³/₄ cup applesauce
1¹/₂ cups flour
1 cup sugar
¹/₄ cup raisins
¹/₄ cup water
1 tsp. baking soda
³/₄ tsp. salt
¹/₄ tsp. cinnamon
¹/₈ tsp. ground cloves
¹/₈ tsp. ground allspice
¹/₂ tsp. baking powder
3 egg whites

Preheat oven to 350 degrees. Spray a 9" x 9" x 2" pan with a non-fat cooking spray. Combine all but raisins in a medium size bowl. Mix with electric mixer on high for 3 minutes.

Pour mixture into prepared pan and add raisins. Bake 30-35 minutes. Cut while warm.

Yield: 9 servings   Calories: 190   Fat: 1 gram

♥ Soft Chocolate Cherry Cookies ♥

It doesn't get any easier than this!

1 box Lovin' Lites Devils Food Cake mix
1¹/₂ cup lite cherry pie filling
1 tsp. almond extract
¹/₂ cup chocolate chips - if desired

Mix all ingredients well by hand. Drop by teaspoonfuls onto a cookie sheet that has been sprayed with a non-fat cooking spray. Bake at 350 degrees for 10 minutes. Remove from cookie sheet and let cool before frosting. (Frost with creamy fat-free chocolate frosting, if desired.) Do not store in airtight container - they may get too soft.

Yield: 4 dozen   Calories: 40   Fat: 1 gram
(Per cookie w/o frosting or chocolate chips)

DO WHAT YOU WANT TO DO BUT ARE AFRAID TO DO,
TO OBTAIN WHAT YOU KNOW YOU ARE ABLE TO BE.

♥♥♥♥♥♥♥♥♥♥♥♥♥♥♥♥♥♥♥♥♥♥♥♥♥♥♥♥

♥ *Mincemeat Squares* ♥

A nice change instead of mincemeat pie for the holidays. A tasty treat anytime of the year!

9 oz. condensed mincemeat (I use "Borden" brand)
1¹/₂ cups water

Crumble mincemeat into 1¹/₂ cups water. Bring to a brisk boil and boil for one minute. Set aside. (If you prefer you can purchase the already prepared filling in a jar. Use two cups.)

Spray a 9" x 13" pan with a non-fat cooking spray. Set aside.

In medium size bowl mix well with blender:
   2 cups Jiffy Mix
   ¹/₄ cup Nutra-Sweet® Spoonful™ } (OR ¹/₂ c. sugar)
   ¹/₄ cup sugar
   2 egg whites
   4 oz. fat-free cream cheese

Dough will be stiff. Press dough into bottom of pan, covering it completely. Spread prepared mincemeat evenly over dough. With fork punch lots of holes through this dessert before baking. (To allow some of the juices to seep through the crust.)

Bake at 400 degrees for 27-30 minutes.

Let dessert cool. Prepare 1 envelope of Dream Whip as directed on box. Spread evenly over cooled baked mincemeat dessert. Cut into 24 squares.

Yield: 24 servings
   With sugar and Nutra-Sweet® Spoonful™: Calories: 101
                                          Fat: 1.32 grams
   With sugar only: Calories: 109   Fat: 1.32 grams

IT TAKES COURAGE TO STAND UP FOR WHAT IS RIGHT.

♥♥♥♥♥♥♥♥♥♥♥♥♥♥♥♥♥♥♥♥♥♥♥♥♥♥♥

♥♥♥♥♥♥♥♥♥♥♥♥♥♥♥♥♥♥♥♥♥♥♥♥♥♥

♥ *Fruit Filled Snack Squares* ♥

1 box Pillsbury Lovin' Lites White Cake mix
$^1/_2$ cup rolled oats
1 tsp. cinnamon
$^1/_3$ cup applesauce
2 Tbs. skim milk
2 egg whites

Filling:
   1 - 20 oz. can of your favorite "Lite" pie filling (blueberry,
   cherry or apple)

Topping:
   $^1/_2$ cup rolled oats
   $^1/_2$ tsp. cinnamon

Combine top 6 ingredients listed. Beat on low speed until
crumbly. Set aside 1 cup of this mixture for later. Press
remaining mixture into a 9" x 13" pan that's been sprayed
with a non-fat cooking spray. Bake at 350 degrees for 15
minutes or until golden brown.

Spread pie filling over crust. Combine the 1 cup of mixture set
aside earlier with $^1/_2$ cup rolled oats and $^1/_2$ tsp. cinnamon.
With fingers put little dabs of this mixture all over top of pie
filling. Bake an additional 23-25 minutes until top is golden
brown and pie filling is bubbly.

Cool completely before cutting.

Yield: 24 servings   Calories: 104   Fat: 1.66 grams

WE HAVE ONE RULE FOR OUR HOME: "LOVE ONLY". IF
IT'S NOT LOVING THEN DON'T DO IT.

♥♥♥♥♥♥♥♥♥♥♥♥♥♥♥♥♥♥♥♥♥♥♥♥♥

♥♥♥♥♥♥♥♥♥♥♥♥♥♥♥♥♥♥♥♥♥♥♥♥♥

♥ *Pumpkin Bars* ♥

2 tsp. cinnamon
1 tsp. pumpkin pie spice
$^1/_2$ cup brown sugar
1 cup pumpkin (from a can)
1 box super moist white cake mix (with pudding in the
    mix) I use Betty Crocker

Mix all ingredients with blender until well mixed. Dough will
be stiff.

Spread with a knife into a 9" x 13" pan that has been sprayed
with a non-fat cooking spray. Set aside.

Topping:
   $^1/_2$ cup quick cooking rolled oats
   $^1/_2$ cup brown sugar
   1 tsp. pumpkin pie spice
   $^1/_4$ cup all purpose flour
   $^1/_4$ cup Ultra Fat-Free Promise Margarine

With a fork, stir margarine into all ingredients until well
blended. Using 2 forks (one fork to push topping off the other
fork), spread topping over pumpkin mixture. There will be
some spaces where you can see the pumpkin mixture.

Bake at 350 degrees for 30 minutes or until knife inserted in
center comes out clean.

Glaze (optional):
   $^1/_4$ cup powdered sugar
   $^1/_2$ tsp. pumpkin pie spice
   $2^1/_2$ - 3 tsp. milk

Drizzle glaze over bars once they have cooled.

Yield: 18 servings   Calories: 155
Fat: 1.8 grams

MORE IMPORTANT THAN HOW MUCH MONEY WE
MAKE IS WHAT WE DO WITH THE MONEY WE MAKE.

♥♥♥♥♥♥♥♥♥♥♥♥♥♥♥♥♥♥♥♥♥♥♥♥♥

♥♥♥♥♥♥♥♥♥♥♥♥♥♥♥♥♥♥♥♥♥♥♥♥♥♥♥♥♥

♥ *Fruit Pizzas (Two)* ♥

2³/₄ cups buttermilk pancake mix
¹/₂ cup sugar
8 oz. fat-free cream cheese (softened)
¹/₃ cup Nutra-Sweet® Spoonful™ (<u>OR</u> ¹/₃ c. sugar)
¹/₂ cup water

Beat until all ingredients are well blended. Spray cookie sheets
with non-fat cooking spray. Press dough with palms to cover
bottom of pans. Bake 350 degrees for 7-10 minutes, until
golden brown. Use 2 - 13¹/₄" x 9¹/₄" cookie sheets.

Frosting:
   ¹/₂ cup Nutra-Sweet® Spoonful™ (<u>OR</u> ¹/₂ c. sugar)
   1 tsp. almond extract
   2 - 8 oz. fat-free cream cheese - softened
   2 Tbs. maraschino cherry juice (drain juice from a jar of
      maraschino cherries)

Decorate with your choice of fresh fruit. I like to use kiwi,
strawberries, grapes and oranges.

Yield: 24 servings
   With Nutra-Sweet® Spoonful™: Calories: 87   Fat: 0.3 grams
   With sugar: Calories: 113   Fat: 0.3 grams

UNFORTUNATELY MANY PEOPLE ARE CONTENT BEING
DISCONTENT AND HAPPY BEING UNHAPPY.

♥♥♥♥♥♥♥♥♥♥♥♥♥♥♥♥♥♥♥♥♥♥♥♥♥♥♥♥♥

❤ *No-Fat Pumpkin Cookies* ❤

1 cup applesauce
1 pkg. Butter Buds - dry (do not dilute)
½ cup brown sugar
2 Tbs. Sugar Twin Brown Sugar Replacement
1 cup canned pumpkin
1 cup all-purpose flour
1 cup whole wheat flour
1 tsp. baking soda
1 tsp. cinnamon
¼ tsp. ginger
¼ tsp. ground cloves
½ tsp. lite salt

Mix first five ingredients well. Add remaining ingredients, mix well. Drop by teaspoonfuls onto cookie sheets that have been sprayed with a non-fat cooking spray.

Bake 375 degrees for 10-12 minutes.

Once removed from oven spray tops lightly with non-fat cooking spray. Gently press top of each cookie into topping.

Topping:
3 Tbs. Nutra-Sweet + 1 Tbs. cinnamon

Yield: 24 servings   Calories: 58   Fat: 0.2

IF YOU DON'T AT LEAST TRY TO DO SOMETHING
YOU'VE ALWAYS WANTED TO DO,
YOU'LL ALWAYS WISH YOU WOULD HAVE.

♥♥♥♥♥♥♥♥♥♥♥♥♥♥♥♥♥♥♥♥♥♥♥♥♥♥♥♥

♥ *Chocolate Chip Cookies* (The Healthy Ones!) ♥

1 pkg. Butter Buds - dry
1/4 cup lite corn syrup
1/2 cup sugar
1/4 cup Nutra Sweet® Spoonful™   } (OR 3/4 c. sugar)
5 egg whites
1 tsp. vanilla
1 cup all purpose flour
1 cup whole wheat flour
1 cup bran (I use oat bran)
1 tsp. baking soda
1 tsp. lite salt
1 pkg. (11.5 oz. size) chocolate chips (I use milk chocolate)

Mix first 6 ingredients; beat well for a minute with mixer. Add remaining ingredients except chocolate chips. Mix well. Add chocolate chips.

Spray cookie sheets with a non-fat cooking spray. Drop by rounded teaspoonfulls onto cookie sheets. Bake at 425 degrees for 8 minutes.

Yield: 3 dozen cookies
　　With sugar and Nutra Sweet® Spoonful™: Calories: 75 each
　　　　　　　　　　　　　　　　　　　　Fat: 1.7 grams each
　　With sugar only: Calories: 80 each　Fat: 1.7 grams each

♥ *Chewy-Gooey No Bake Freezer Cookies* ♥

This cookie, like a frozen dessert, will melt. It can NOT be left out to thaw. It must be eaten IMMEDIATELY once removed from the freezer.

2 cups sugar
1/2 cup skim milk
1/4 cup Fat-Free Ultra Promise Margarine
3 Tbs. cocoa
1 tsp. vanilla
1/2 cup fat-free cream cheese
3 cups quick cooking oats

Combine first 4 ingredients in 2 quart saucepan. Stirring constantly. Bring to a full boil for 1 minute. Remove from heat, add vanilla, cream cheese and stir until well blended. Add oats.

Drop onto wax paper by teaspoon. Keep in freezer until ready to eat.

Yield: 3 dozen　　　　Calories: 60　　　　Fat: 0.3 grams
♥♥♥♥♥♥♥♥♥♥♥♥♥♥♥♥♥♥♥♥♥♥♥♥♥♥♥

♥♥♥♥♥♥♥♥♥♥♥♥♥♥♥♥♥♥♥♥♥♥♥♥♥♥♥♥♥

♥ *Harvest Cookies* ♥

1/2 tsp. vanilla
1/4 cup applesauce
3/4 cup brown sugar
1/2 cup Nutra Sweet® Spoonful™ (<u>OR</u> 1/2 c. sugar)
4 egg whites
2 cups whole wheat flour
1 tsp. baking soda
1/2 tsp. lite salt
1 tsp. cinnamon
1/2 tsp. ground cloves or nutmeg
1/2 cup chopped nuts (optional)
2 medium apples - peeled and chopped (approximately 1
    cup)

Beat egg whites until foamy. Mix egg whites with Nutra-Sweet, brown sugar, applesauce and vanilla. Stir in baking soda, salt, cinnamon, ground cloves (or nutmeg) until well mixed. Stir in whole wheat flour, one cup at a time. Mix until well blended. Stir in chopped apples (and nuts if desired).

By teaspoonfuls put onto cookie sheet sprayed with a non-fat spray. Bake at 375 degrees for 5-6 minutes. (Until bottoms are golden brown.)

Yield: 4 1/2 - 5 dozen
   With Nutra Sweet® Spoonful™: Calories: 34   Fat: .75 grams
   With sugar: Calories: 40   Fat: .75

WOULDN'T IT BE WONDERFUL IF EVERYONE IN THE
WORLD WAS AS FAST TO COMPLIMENT AS THEY ARE
TO CRITICIZE.

♥♥♥♥♥♥♥♥♥♥♥♥♥♥♥♥♥♥♥♥♥♥♥♥♥♥♥♥♥

♥♥♥♥♥♥♥♥♥♥♥♥♥♥♥♥♥♥♥♥♥♥♥♥♥♥♥♥

♥ *Chocolate Cookies* ♥

2¹/₂ cups flour
1¹/₂ cups sugar
¹/₂ cup Nutra Sweet® Spoonful™
4 cups quick cooking oats
1¹/₃ cups cocoa
1 Tbs. + 1 tsp. baking powder
1 tsp. lite salt
16 egg whites
¹/₃ cup lite corn syrup
¹/₃ cup applesauce
1 Tbs. + 1 tsp. vanilla

} (**OR** 2 c. sugar)

Beat egg whites with baking powder, salt, applesauce and corn syrup until bubbly and lightly foamy. Add remaining dry ingredients. Mix well.

Drop by teaspoonfuls onto cookie sheet that has been sprayed with a non-fat spray.

Bake at 350 degrees for 9 minutes. Remove cookies from cookie sheet immediately. Store in air tight container once cooled.

Yield: 8 doz. cookies (1 cookie per serving)
    With sugar and Nutra Sweet® Spoonful™: Calories: 56 each
                                          Fat: 1.2 grams each
        With sugar only: Calories: 60 each   Fat: 1.2 grams each

Chocolate chunk cookies: Add 1 - 10 oz. bag of semi-sweet chocolate chunks.

Yield: 8 doz. cookies   Calories: 42 each cookie
                                   Fat: 1.2 grams per cookie

Chocolate raisin cookies: Add 2 cups of raisins and 1 - 10 oz. bag of chocolate chunks.

Yield: 8 doz. cookies (1 cookie per serving)
    With sugar and Nutra Sweet® Spoonful™: Calories: 65 each
                                          Fat: 1.2 grams each
        With sugar only: Calories: 69 each   Fat: 1.2 grams each

I BELIEVE NO ONE CAN KNOW TRUE LOVE, UNLESS THEY
ALSO KNOW GOD.

♥♥♥♥♥♥♥♥♥♥♥♥♥♥♥♥♥♥♥♥♥♥♥♥♥♥♥♥

❤❤❤❤❤❤❤❤❤❤❤❤❤❤❤❤❤❤❤❤❤❤❤❤❤

❤ *Two-In-One Chocolate Sandwich Cookie* ❤

6 egg whites
¹/₄ cup applesauce
¹/₄ cup corn syrup
2 tsp. vanilla
1¹/₄ cup evaporated skim milk

Beat egg whites. Add remaining ingredients. Mix well.

Once mixed well, add dry ingredients.

2 cups whole wheat flour
1¹/₄ cups all purpose flour
1 cup sugar
¹/₂ cup + 2 Tbs. Nutra Sweet® Spoonful™   } (OR 1¹/₂ c. sugar + 2 Tbs. sugar)
1 cup unsweetened cocoa powder
¹/₂ cup cornstarch
1 Tbs. baking powder
1 tsp. baking soda
1¹/₂ tsp. lite salt

Mix together well in large bowl.

For a plain cookie: (By teaspoon put onto cookie sheet that has been sprayed with a no-fat spray.) Bake at 350 degrees for 5 minutes or until done.

Yield: 4 dozen cookies (1 cookie per serving)
    With sugar and Nutra Sweet® Spoonful™: Calories: 71 each
                                            Fat: 0.4 grams each
    With sugar only: Calories: 81 each   Fat: 0.4 grams each

For an ice cream sandwich: Once cooled add 1 rounded tablespoon of your favorite no-fat frozen yogurt between two cookies to make a sandwich. MMM! MMM!

Yield: 2 dozen cookies (1 cookie per serving)
    With sugar and Nutra Sweet® Spoonful™: Calories: 157 each
                                            Fat: 0.8 grams each
    With sugar only: Calories: 177 each   Fat: 0.8 grams each

EXERCISE YOUR NOSE. TAKE TIME TO SMELL THE
FLOWERS.

❤❤❤❤❤❤❤❤❤❤❤❤❤❤❤❤❤❤❤❤❤❤❤❤❤

Two-In-One Chocolate Sandwich Cookie (continued)

For a sandwich cookie: Between two cookies put a dab of marshmallow creme.

Yield: 2 dozen cookies (1 cookie per serving)
   With sugar and Nutra Sweet® Spoonful™: Calories: 149 each
                                           Fat: 0.8 grams each
     With sugar only: Calories: 169 each   Fat: 0.8 grams each

♥ *Spicy Raisin Cookies* ♥

1 cup applebutter (use your favorite brand)
1 cup dark brown sugar
$^1/_2$ cup Nutra Sweet® Spoonful™ (OR $^1/_2$ c. sugar)
6 egg whites
1 tsp. vanilla
1 tsp. baking soda
1 tsp. lite salt
1 tsp. cinnamon
$^1/_2$ tsp. ground cloves
2 cups whole wheat flour
1 cup self-rising flour
2 cups raisins
$^1/_3$ cup chopped pecans

Beat first nine ingredients together at medium speed until well blended. Add both kinds of flour, one cup at a time. By hand stir in raisins and pecans. Drop by teaspoonful onto cookie sheet sprayed with no-fat spray.

Bake at 375 degrees for 7 minutes. Makes 6 dozen.

Glaze:
    $^1/_2$ cup dark brown sugar
    $^1/_2$ cup Healthy Choice fat-free cream cheese
    1 tsp. vanilla

Blend well. Quickly put a thin layer of glaze on cookies while they are still warm.

Yield: 72 servings (1 cookie per serving)
   With Nutra Sweet® Spoonful™: Calories: 47   Fat: 0.4 grams
   With sugar: Calories: 52   Fat: 0.4 grams

KNOW WHEN TO KEEP YOUR MOUTH SHUT.

♥♥♥♥♥♥♥♥♥♥♥♥♥♥♥♥♥♥♥♥♥♥♥♥♥♥♥

♥♥♥♥♥♥♥♥♥♥♥♥♥♥♥♥♥♥♥♥♥♥♥♥♥♥

❤ *Itty Bitty Tea Cookies* ❤

Crust:
> 1¹/₃ cup buttermilk pancake mix ⎫
> ¹/₄ cup sugar   ⎬ (OR ¹/₃ c. sugar)
> 2 Tbs. Nutra Sweet® Spoonful™   ⎭
> ¹/₄ cup juice from maraschino cherries
> 4 oz. fat-free cream cheese

Beat together well until blended. Spray cookie sheet (9¹/₄" x 13¹/₄") with a non-fat cooking spray. With palm, press dough to cover bottom of pan, to edges of pan.

Bake at 350 degrees for 7-10 minutes.

Frosting:
> ¹/₂ tsp. almond extract
> ¹/₄ cup Nutra Sweet® Spoonful™ (OR ¹/₄ c. sugar)
> 8 oz. fat-free cream cheese - softened
> 1 Tbs. maraschino cherry juice (drain from a jar of
>   maraschino cherries)

Beat until smooth and creamy. Frost large cookie (after cookie has cooled.) After frosted cut into 63 small pieces. Cut 32 maraschino cherries in half. Place cherry half in each square.

> 2 Tbs. fat-free hot fudge (I use Smuckers)
> 1 tsp. maraschino cherry juice

Mix and warm hot fudge and cherry juice. Drizzle, with spoon, over cookies.

Yield: 63 servings (1 cookie per serving)
>   With Nutra Sweet® Spoonful™: Calories: 17 each
>   Fat: 0.1 grams each
>   With sugar: Calories: 23   Fat: 0.1 grams each

DON'T EAT YOUR BLUES AWAY.
IT'S OKAY TO FEEL SAD, OR LONELY.

♥♥♥♥♥♥♥♥♥♥♥♥♥♥♥♥♥♥♥♥♥♥♥♥♥♥

♥ *Chocolate Banana Chocolate Pie* ♥

8 oz. chocolate cream sandwich cookies (I use
  Snackwell's)
3 Tbs. liquid Butter Buds
$^1/_2$ tsp. Nutra Sweet® Spoonful™
2 quarts of no-fat chocolate frozen yogurt (set out to thaw
  while making pie crust)
3 bananas (sliced into $^1/_4$" thickness)
1 - 11.5 oz. fat free Smucker's hot fudge topping
$^1/_3$ cup cocoa
$^1/_3$ cup powdered sugar
1 - 8 oz. carton of light Cool Whip
2 Tbs. chocolate chips (optional)

Pie Crust: Remove and discard cream filling from chocolate
sandwich cookies. Put cookies into food processor and process
until cookies are fine crumbs. Put crumbs in bowl along with 3
Tbs. liquid Butter Buds and $^1/_2$ tsp. Nutra Sweet® Spoonful™;
mix well with fork. Spray 9" pie pan with no-fat cooking
spray. Press cookie mixture into pie pan. (Press along sides of
pan also.)

Arrange the banana slices on bottom of pie crust. Spoon as
much as possible of the no-fat chocolate frozen yogurt, that
has been slightly thawed, into pie crust over bananas. Spoon
about $^2/_3$ of Smucker's fat-free hot fudge topping on top.
Sprinkle with 2 Tbs. chocolate chips.

Melt remaining hot fudge in microwave and drizzle over pie.
Keep frozen until ready to serve.

Although this is low fat it's loaded with calories so beware!
When eating this special treat remember moderation is the
name of this game.

Yield: 10 servings   Calories: 311   Fat: 2.7 grams

THE GREATEST GIFT IN LIFE IS TO LOVE
AND TO BE LOVED.

♥♥♥♥♥♥♥♥♥♥♥♥♥♥♥♥♥♥♥♥♥♥♥♥♥♥

♥ Cherry Cobbler ♥

2 cups pie cherries, cleaned & pitted
$^1/_2$ cup sugar
$^1/_4$ cup Nutra Sweet® Spoonful™ } (OR $^3/_4$ c. sugar)
1 tsp. cinnamon

Mix pie cherries with Nutra Sweet® Spoonful™ & cinnamon.
Put into 9" x 13" baking pan.

2 cups Hungry Jack Pillsbury buttermilk pancake/waffle
    mix - dry
$^1/_4$ cup Nutra Sweet® Spoonful™
$^2/_3$ cup water

Mix together well. Dough will be lumpy. With a fork put
dough on top of cherry mixture.

Bake approximately 30-35 minutes at 350 degrees. (Cherries
are bubbly and dough golden brown when done.)

Yield: 12 servings
        With sugar and Nutra Sweet® Spoonful™: Calories: 114
                                                Fat: 0.6 grams
        With sugar only: Calories: 146   Fat: 0.6 grams

♥ Chocolate Cherry Brownies ♥

2 boxes of Lovin' Lites Brownie Mix
1 can lite cherry pie filling
2 egg whites
$^1/_2$ cup chocolate chips

Mix all ingredients together by hand, about 75 strokes or until
well blended.

Spray 2 - 9" x 13" pans with a non-fat cooking spray. Spread
batter into prepared pans. Bake at 350 degrees for 25-27
minutes.

Immediately after taken out of oven sprinkle each pan with a
$^1/_4$ cup of chocolate chips. Cut each pan into 16 pieces.

Yield: 32 servings   Calories: 161   Fat: 2.3 grams

THE BEST REMEDY FOR DISCONTENTMENT IS TO LOOK
AT ALL WE HAVE TO BE THANKFUL FOR.

♥♥♥♥♥♥♥♥♥♥♥♥♥♥♥♥♥♥♥♥♥♥♥♥♥♥

♥♥♥♥♥♥♥♥♥♥♥♥♥♥♥♥♥♥♥♥♥♥♥♥♥♥♥

♥ *Blueberry Cobbler* ♥

2 cups blueberries
⅓ cup sugar
1 tsp. almond extract
½ tsp. orange peel
2 cups Hungry Jack Pillsbury buttermilk pancake/waffle
    mix - dry
¼ cup Nutra Sweet® Spoonful™ (<u>OR</u> ¼ c. sugar)
⅔ cup water

Gently stir sugar and orange peel together to coat blueberries.
Put into a 9" x 13" baking pan.

Mix pancake mix, Nutra-Sweet, water and almond extract
together. Dough will be lumpy. With a fork put dough on top
of blueberry mixture.

Bake approximately 30-35 minutes at 350 degrees.
(Blueberries are bubbly and dough golden brown when done.)

Yield: 12 servings
        With sugar and Nutra Sweet® Spoonful™: Calories: 97
                                            Fat: 0.6 grams
            With sugar only: Calories: 112   Fat: 0.6 grams

♥♥♥♥♥♥♥♥♥♥♥♥♥♥♥♥♥♥♥♥♥♥♥♥♥♥

♥♥♥♥♥♥♥♥♥♥♥♥♥♥♥♥♥♥♥♥♥♥♥♥♥♥♥

♥ *Creamy Spiced Whipped Topping* ♥

1 pkg. of Dream Whip (a box comes with 4 pkgs.)
$^1/_2$ cup cold skim milk
$^1/_2$ tsp. cinnamon
$^1/_2$ tsp. ground cloves

Beat on high for 4 minutes. Keep refrigerated until ready to
eat. If you're going to frost the cake, refrigerate the whole
cake once frosted.

Yield: 16 servings (2 Tbs. each)
Calories: 18   Fat: 0.55 grams

♥ *Blackberry Cobbler* ♥
Super Easy, Super Yummy

2 quarts blackberries
$^1/_2$ cup sugar
$^1/_4$ cup Nutra Sweet® Spoonful™ } (<u>OR</u> $^3/_4$ c. sugar)
1 tsp. cinnamon
$^1/_3$ cup sugar
2 Tbs. Nutra Sweet® Spoonful™ } (<u>OR</u> $^1/_2$ c. sugar)

Take 2 quarts blackberries and gently mix with a $^1/_2$ cup sugar
and a $^1/_4$ cup Nutra Sweet® Spoonful™. Put in a 9" x 13" pan.
Sprinkle 1 tsp. cinnamon on top of sugared berries. Using 2
cups of "Staff Brand" pancake mix, $^1/_3$ cup sugar, 2 Tbs. Nutra
Sweet® Spoonful™ and stir with enough water to make stiff
dough. With fork spread on top of berries.

Bake 30-35 minutes at 350 degrees. (Berries will be bubbly
and dough golden brown when done.)

Yield: 12 servings
        With sugar and Nutra Sweet® Spoonful™: Calories: 116
                                        Fat: 0.4 grams
        With sugar only: Calories: 138   Fat: 0.4 grams

♥♥♥♥♥♥♥♥♥♥♥♥♥♥♥♥♥♥♥♥♥♥♥♥♥♥♥

♥♥♥♥♥♥♥♥♥♥♥♥♥♥♥♥♥♥♥♥♥♥♥♥♥

♥ *Fruit Topped Cheesecake* ♥

1 box Lovin' Lites yellow cake mix
2 Tbs. applesauce
2 - 8 oz. packages fat-free cream cheese - softened
8 egg whites
1½ cups skim milk
3 Tbs. vanilla
2 Tbs. lemon juice
1 - 21 oz. can lite pie filling (cherry or blueberry)
¼ cup + 1 Tbs. sugar   } (OR ½ c. sugar minus 1
2 Tbs. Nutra Sweet® Spoonful™ } Tbs. sugar)

Set aside 1 cup of dry cake mix. In large bowl mix remaining cake mix, 2 egg whites and applesauce. Spray 9" x 13" pan with no-fat cooking spray. Press this mixture onto bottom of pan evenly.

Mix together Nutra Sweet® Spoonful™, sugar and softened cream cheese. Add 6 egg whites and reserved dry cake mix. Beat 1 minute at medium speed. Add milk, vanilla and lemon juice. Mix until smooth. Pour on top of pressed mixture in pan. Bake at 300 degrees for 65-75 minutes, or until center is firm. Once cooled, top with pie filling. Chill before serving. Keep refrigerated.

Yield: 16 servings
    With sugar and Nutra Sweet® Spoonful™: Calories: 168
                                        Fat: 1.6 grams
        With sugar only: Calories: 189   Fat: 1.6 grams

**THOSE WHO ARE THANKFUL FOR THE LITTLE THINGS
ARE THE ONES WHO ENJOY LIFE TO THE FULLEST.**

♥♥♥♥♥♥♥♥♥♥♥♥♥♥♥♥♥♥♥♥♥♥♥♥♥

♥♥♥♥♥♥♥♥♥♥♥♥♥♥♥♥♥♥♥♥♥♥♥♥♥♥

♥ Lazette's Luscious Strawberry Cheesecake ♥

2 - 8 oz. fat-free cream cheese
1 - 8 oz. fat-free sour cream
1 - 8 oz. fat-free Cool Whip
$^3/_4$ cup confectioner's sugar } (OR 1$^1/_4$ c. confectioner's
$^1/_2$ cup Nutra Sweet® Spoonful™ } sugar)
2 tsp. vanilla
1 tsp. almond flavoring
1 - 10 oz. angel food cake
2 quarts of strawberries
$^1/_4$ cup Nutra Sweet® Spoonful™ (OR $^1/_4$ c. sugar) to
   sweeten berries

Beat cream cheese until softened. Beat in sour cream. Stir in lite Cool Whip, confectioner's sugar, vanilla and almond flavoring (also add $^1/_2$ c. Nutra Sweet® Spoonful™ if using the Nutra Sweet® Spoonful™ recipe). Cut angel food cake into 2" pieces. Sweeten berries with $^1/_4$ Nutra Sweet® Spoonful™ (or $^1/_4$ c. sugar).

Layer cream mixture and strawberries in deep glass bowl. Garnish top with whole berries.

Yield: 20 servings
   With Nutra Sweet® Spoonful™: Calories: 132 Fat: 1.0 grams
   With sugar only: Calories: 152   Fat: 1.0 grams

♥ Cherry Trifle ♥

1 can Lite Cherry Pie filling
Beat together:
     1 cup powdered sugar
     8 oz. no-fat cream cheese
Add: 8 oz. non-dairy whipped topping
Add: $^1/_4$ cup chopped pecans or walnuts
Stir in: 5 cups cubed angel food cake

Layer in glass bowl:
     $^1/_2$ cake mixture
     $^1/_2$ can cherry pie filling

Repeat until all ingredients have been used. Chill for at least 3 hours before serving.

Yield: 15 servings   Calories: 168   Fat: 1.6 grams

♥♥♥♥♥♥♥♥♥♥♥♥♥♥♥♥♥♥♥♥♥♥♥♥♥

❤ Three Layer Chocolate Mint Cake ❤

Seeing the pretty light green frosting between the layers makes this an extra special beauty!

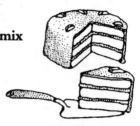

1 tsp. chocolate sprinkles (optional)
1 pkg. devils food Lovin' Lites cake mix
1 1/2 cups cold skim milk
3 pkgs. Dream Whip
1/4 cup cocoa - sifted
1/3 cup powdered sugar - sifted
green food coloring
peppermint extract

Preheat oven to 350 degrees. Make cake as directed on package. Pour into 3 - 10" cake pans that have been sprayed with a non-fat spray. Bake approximately 12 minutes or until knife inserted in center comes out clean.

Beat 3 packs of Dream Whip with 1 1/2 cups cold skim milk until peaks form. Take 1/3 of prepared Dream Whip and put into small bowl. Add 1/2 tsp. peppermint extract and 3 drops green food coloring. Mix until well blended. Put in refrigerator until cake is ready to be frosted.

With remaining 2/3 of prepared Dream Whip add cocoa, powdered sugar and 1/2 tsp. of peppermint extract.

After cake is cooled completely, put first of the 3 baked layers on a cake plate. Frost with 1/2 of the light green colored prepared Dream Whip. Put 2nd layer of cake on top. Frost with the remaining light green colored prepared Dream Whip. Put 3rd layer of cake on top. Frost sides of cake with chocolate colored prepared Dream Whip, then frost top of cake last.

Sprinkle 1 teaspoon chocolate sprinkles on top of cake (optional).

Cover and keep refrigerated until ready to serve.

| Yield: 12 servings | Calories: 196 | Fat: 2.9 grams |

ALWAYS SHOW APPRECIATION.

♥♥♥♥♥♥♥♥♥♥♥♥♥♥♥♥♥♥♥♥♥♥♥♥♥♥♥♥

♥ *Daddy's Favorite Peach Spice Cake* ♥

This is my husband's favorite cake.

1¹/₂ cups applesauce
3 cups wheat flour
1 cup sugar
1 cup brown sugar
¹/₂ cup water
2 tsp. baking soda
1¹/₂ tsp. lite salt
¹/₂ tsp. cinnamon
¹/₄ tsp. ground cloves
¹/₄ tsp. ground allspice
1 tsp. baking powder
6 egg whites
1 - 29 oz. can sliced peaches - drained

Preheat oven to 350 degrees. Spray a 9" x 13" pan with a non-fat spray. Combine all ingredients in a large bowl. Mix with electric mixer for 3 minutes, scraping sides of bowl often.

Pour mixture into prepared pan. Arrange sliced peaches on top of batter pressing each peach slice down so that top of each peach shows and ¹/₂ of the peach slice is in batter.

Bake 37-47 minutes or until knife inserted in middle comes out clean. Cut while warm.

Spicy whipped topping: Make 2 Dream Whip packages as directed. Add 1 tsp. cinnamon and ¹/₂ tsp. allspice. Blend into topping. Spoon topping onto cake.

Yield: 24 servings   Calories: 130   Fat: 2.0 grams

NO ONE HAS THE RIGHT TO DO ONLY AS HE PLEASES
UNLESS HE ONLY PLEASES TO DO RIGHT BY GOD.

♥♥♥♥♥♥♥♥♥♥♥♥♥♥♥♥♥♥♥♥♥♥♥♥♥♥♥♥

♥♥♥♥♥♥♥♥♥♥♥♥♥♥♥♥♥♥♥♥♥♥♥♥♥♥♥♥

♥ *Very Berry Cake* ♥

1 cup frozen or fresh berries (I used black raspberries)
1 Tbs. Nutra Sweet® Spoonful™
¼ cup sugar   } (OR ⅓ c. sugar)
½ Tbs. lemon juice

Toss berries with Nutra Sweet® Spoonful™. Heat sugar and
lemon juice in sauce pan until sugar is dissolved.

Spray 8" or 9" round cake pan with a non-fat cooking spray.
Arrange berries in pan evenly. Pour dissolved sugar/lemon
mixture over berries.

½ cup whole wheat flour
½ cup all purpose flour
⅓ cup sugar
3 Tbs. Nutra Sweet® Spoonful™ } (OR ½ c. sugar)
2 tsp. baking powder
½ tsp. lite salt
4 egg whites
½ cup water
⅓ cup applesauce
1 tsp. vanilla

Mix all ingredients above by hand until smooth. Carefully pour
cake batter over berries. Bake 30 minutes or until toothpick
inserted in center comes out clean.

As soon as you take cake out of oven run knife around outer
edge of cake pan and invert cake onto serving plate.

This cake can be frozen then put into the microwave and
served warm with Dream Whip, no-fat frozen vanilla yogurt or
Cool Whip.

Yield: 16 servings
　　　With sugar and Nutra Sweet® Spoonful™: Calories: 151
　　　　　　　　　　　　　　　　　　　　　Fat: 1.9 grams
　　　With sugar only: Calories: 155　　　　Fat: 1.9 grams

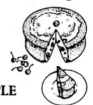

DON'T HANG AROUND PEOPLE
WHO BRING YOU DOWN.
♥♥♥♥♥♥♥♥♥♥♥♥♥♥♥♥♥♥♥♥♥♥♥♥♥♥♥

❤❤❤❤❤❤❤❤❤❤❤❤❤❤❤❤❤❤❤❤❤❤❤❤❤

❤ *Pineapple Up-side Down Cake* ❤

1 - 20 oz. can crushed pineapple - in its own juice
$^1/_4$ cup fat-free Ultra Promise margarine
12 maraschino cherries - cut in $^1/_2$
1 cup dark brown sugar - packed
1 box lite white cake mix (I use Betty Crocker's Super
    Moist)
3 egg whites

Drain as much juice from pineapple as possible. Beat egg
whites, pineapple juice and cake mix for 30 seconds on low,
then 2 minutes on medium speed. Set aside.

Melt fat-free margarine and brown sugar over low heat in
medium size pan until smooth and creamy.

Spray a 9" x 13" pan with non-fat spray. Pour melted sugar
and margarine mixture into pan so that the whole bottom of
pan is covered. With fingers press crushed pineapple and
maraschino cherries into sugar/margarine mixture. Pour
prepared cake batter over pineapple and cherries.

Bake at 350 degrees for 35 minutes or until knife inserted in
middle comes out clean and top of cake is golden brown.
Immediately run spatula around edge of pan.

Cool in pan for 5 minutes. Invert onto a plate.

Yield: 12-16 servings   Calories: 151   Fat: 1.9 grams

I WAS BORN TO HAVE A MAID.

❤❤❤❤❤❤❤❤❤❤❤❤❤❤❤❤❤❤❤❤❤❤❤❤❤

♥ A+ Pumpkin Cake ♥

This cake is absolutely delicious served warm with a glop of creamy spiced whipped topping on each piece. Or once cooled you can frost the cake with the same creamy spiced whipped topping. Keep the cake refrigerated. It's excellent served chilled also!

4 egg whites
²/₃ cup light brown sugar
¹/₃ cup Nutra Sweet® Spoonful™ (OR ¹/₃ c. sugar)
1 tsp. ground cinnamon
¹/₂ tsp. nutmeg
¹/₂ tsp. allspice
1 - 16 oz. can of pumpkin
1 box of lite yellow cake mix (I use Betty Crocker's Super Moist)

Beat egg whites 15 seconds. Add brown sugar, Nutra Sweet® Spoonful™, ground cinnamon, nutmeg, allspice and pumpkin. Mix until well blended. Add cake mix. Beat on high for one minute.

Bake at 350 degrees for 37-40 minutes in a 9" x 13" pan.

Yield: 15 servings
　　With Nutra Sweet® Spoonful™: Calories: 169　Fat: 2.1 grams
　　With sugar only: Calories: 185　　　　　　　Fat: 2.1 grams

WE DO OUR CHILDREN AN INJUSTICE IF WE DO NOT HOLD THEM ACCOUNTABLE FOR THEIR ACTIONS.

♥♥♥♥♥♥♥♥♥♥♥♥♥♥♥♥♥♥♥♥♥♥♥♥♥

♥ *Where the Goo Goes* ♥

If you like upside down pineapple cake and cheese cake you'll like this clever combination. I got this idea from my Grandma, Jerri Seibert.

Crust:
> 2 Tbs. sugar
> 1/3 cup Fat-Free Ultra Promise Margarine
> 11 graham crackers (each graham cracker has 4 segments)

Spray a 9" x 13" pan with a non-fat cooking spray. Set aside. With food processor grind up graham crackers until they are fine crumbs. Melt fat-free margarine in microwave. (About 15 seconds). Mix sugar, melted fat-free margarine and graham cracker crumbs together until well blended with fork. Press into prepared 9" x 13" pan. Bake at 350 degrees for 10 minutes. Let cool.

Cream Filling:
> 1 envelope Dream Whip
> 2 - 8 oz. fat-free cream cheese - softened to room
>   temperature (I use Healthy Choice brand)
> 1 tsp. almond extract
> 1/2 cup cold skim milk
> 1/2 cup powdered sugar (or use 1/4 cup Nutra Sweet®
>   Spoonful™ + 2 Tbs. powdered sugar)

With mixer on high, beat 1 envelope Dream Whip with 1/2 cup cold skim milk and almond extract for 4 minutes. Add softened cream cheese and powdered sugar. Smooth cream mixture over cooled crust.

Topping:
1 - 20 oz. can crushed pineapple with its juices, 2T. cornstarch and 3T. dark brown sugar. With whisk, mix well until cornstarch is completely dissolved. Turn on heat to medium. Bring to a boil, stirring occasionally. Boil for 1 minute. Remove from heat. Cool. Spread on top of cheese mixture. Refrigerate for 2 hours before serving.

Yield: 15 servings
> With powdered sugar only: Calories: 163   Fat: 1.5 grams
> With powdered sugar and Nutra Sweet® Spoonful™:
>   Calories: 150   Fat: 1.5 grams

LET THOSE YOU LOVE KNOW IT.

♥♥♥♥♥♥♥♥♥♥♥♥♥♥♥♥♥♥♥♥♥♥♥♥♥

♥♥♥♥♥♥♥♥♥♥♥♥♥♥♥♥♥♥♥♥♥♥♥♥♥♥♥

♥ *Radiant Rhubarb Cake* ♥

If you like rhubarb, you'll love this cake!

3 cups fresh rhubarb - diced into thin ¼" pieces
¾ cup water
1 cup sugar
1 box strawberry Sugar-Free Jello - dry (4 serving size)
1 box light yellow cake mix (I use Betty Crocker Super
    Moist Light)
6 egg whites
1⅓ cup water
2 cups mini marshmallows

Over medium heat in a saucepan bring the rhubarb, ¾ cup
water and sugar to a boil. Boil 3 minutes. Remove from heat.
Add strawberry Jello - dry. (Do not prepare as directed on
box.) Let cool.

Beat egg whites until bubbly - about 1 minute. Add 1⅓ cup
water and box of light cake mix. Beat 2 minutes on medium
speed.

Spray a 9" x 13" pan with a non-fat cooking spray. Arrange
the mini marshmallows on bottom of prepared pan. Evenly
put cake batter over marshmallows. Spoon the slightly cooled
rhubarb on top of cake batter.

Bake at 350 degrees for 40 minutes.

Serve warm or cold. I like it best warm!

(As this bakes the marshmallows will rise to the top of the
cake. No need for frosting.) If serving warm, I like to put a dab
of Lite Cool Whip on it!

Yield: 15 servings   Calories: 242   Fat: 2.40 grams

THE ONLY THING I'M PERFECT AT IS BEING
PERFECTLY IMPERFECT!

♥♥♥♥♥♥♥♥♥♥♥♥♥♥♥♥♥♥♥♥♥♥♥♥♥

❤ No Bake Eclair Cake ❤

I like this best made 2-3 days before eating.

2 envelopes of Dream Whip - prepared as directed
2 - 3.4 oz. boxes of French vanilla pudding (it has to be
French Vanilla!!) - prepared as directed on box
1/2 jar Smuckers Fat-Free Hot Fudge (11.5 oz. size)
whole graham crackers

Prepare both Dream Whip and pudding as directed.
Refrigerate for 5 minutes. Line a 9" x 13" pan with whole
graham crackers. 7 1/2 whole graham crackers (each including 4
sections) will be needed to cover the bottom of the pan.

Mix pudding and Dream Whip together until well blended.
Pour 1/2 of the pudding/Dream Whip mixture on top of graham
crackers. Put another layer of 7 1/2 whole graham crackers on
top of pudding/Dream Whip mixture.

Put remaining pudding/Dream Whip mixture on top of graham
crackers. Put 7 1/2 whole graham crackers on top of pudding/
Dream Whip mixture.

From bottom going up we should have:
graham crackers (7 1/2)
1/2 pudding/Dream Whip mixture
graham crackers (7 1/2)
remaining pudding/Dream Whip mixture
graham crackers (7 1/2)
top with hot fudge

Frost top layer of graham crackers with hot fudge that has
been microwaved for a few seconds, so that it will spread
easier.

Refrigerate. Serve chilled.

Yield: 15 servings   Calories: 222   Fat: 3 grams

♥♥♥♥♥♥♥♥♥♥♥♥♥♥♥♥♥♥♥♥♥♥♥♥♥♥♥

♥ *Carrot Snack Cake* ♥

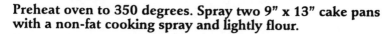

8 egg whites
2 cups dark brown sugar - packed
2 tsp. baking soda
2 tsp. cinnamon
³/₄ tsp. lite salt
1¹/₂ cup applesauce
2 cups flour
2 cups firmly packed coarsely grated carrots
1 cup raisins

Preheat oven to 350 degrees. Spray two 9" x 13" cake pans with a non-fat cooking spray and lightly flour.

With mixer - beat egg whites until foamy - about 1 minute. Gradually beat sugar into egg whites. Beat the baking soda and cinnamon into egg mixture. Beginning and ending with flour mix the flour, applesauce, flour, applesauce and flour into the egg mixture. Fold in carrots and raisins.

Bake 40-50 minutes or until sides of cake are loose from edge of pans. Cool in pans for 10 minutes, then take cakes out of pans and cool completely.

Yield: 15 servings   Calories: 158   Fat: 0.3

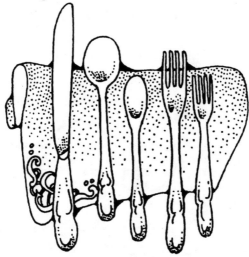

WE SHOULD APPLAUD THE EFFORTS OF PEOPLE, NOT
ONLY THEIR FINAL RESULTS.

♥♥♥♥♥♥♥♥♥♥♥♥♥♥♥♥♥♥♥♥♥♥♥♥♥♥♥

♥♥♥♥♥♥♥♥♥♥♥♥♥♥♥♥♥♥♥♥♥♥♥♥♥♥♥

♥ *Caramel Apple Cakes* (makes 2 cakes) ♥

1 box Lovin' Lites White Cake Mix
2 - 20 oz. cans apple pie filling (one for each cake)
$^1/_2$ cup caramel topping (I use Smucker's brand - fat-free)
$^1/_2$ tsp. cinnamon

Prepare cakes as directed on box. Spray 2 - 9" square or round pans with a no-fat cooking spray. Pour batter into prepared pans.

After baking let cakes sit for 10 minutes once removed from oven. Remove cakes from pan and let cool completely. Cut each cake in $^1/_2$, dividing into two parts (an upper and lower level). Spread $^2/_3$'s can of apple pie filling onto lower half of each cake. Sprinkle with cinnamon.

Top cakes with top cake layers. Spread remaining apple pie filling on top layer of cake. Again sprinkle with cinnamon. Microwave caramel for 10 seconds - just enough so it's of thin consistency. Drizzle caramel over cake - $^1/_4$ cup for each cake.

Yield: 18 servings   Calories: 184   Fat: 1.7

♥ *Sour Cream Chocolate Cake* ♥

1 - 18 oz. box Betty Crocker devil's food light super moist cake mix
6 egg whites
$^1/_2$ cup no-fat sour cream
$^1/_3$ + $^1/_2$ cup cold water

Beat all ingredients on low for three seconds. Beat on medium speed two minutes more.

Spray two 9" round cake pans with a non-fat cooking spray. Divide batter between 2 pans. Bake for 30 minutes (or until cake pulls away from sides of pan and springs back when touched in the center). Cool 10 minutes in pans. Remove from pan. Cool completely.

Frost with fat-free chocolate frosting. (recipe on page 169).

Yield: 12 servings   Calories: 200   Fat: 3 grams

THE GIFT OF LOVE IS MORE VALUABLE THAN MONEY
CAN BUY.

♥♥♥♥♥♥♥♥♥♥♥♥♥♥♥♥♥♥♥♥♥♥♥♥♥♥

Index

Symbols

♥♥♥♥♥♥♥♥♥♥♥♥♥♥♥♥♥♥♥♥♥♥♥♥♥♥♥♥♥

DOWN HOME COOKIN' WITHOUT THE DOWN HOME FAT
COOKBOOK ORDER FORM

ATTENTION: COZY HOMESTEAD, INC.
5425 S. FULTON LUCAS ROAD   ••   SWANTON, OHIO 43558

THESE COOKBOOKS ARE NOT ONLY HEALTHY BUT THEY ALSO
<u>MAKE GREAT GIFTS!!</u>

PLEASE SEND _____ COPIES OF YOUR COOKBOOK AT $9.95
EACH <u>PLUS $2.00 POSTAGE AND HANDLING (FOR EVERY BOOK
ORDERED).</u> ENCLOSED IS MY CHECK PAYABLE TO COZY
HOMESTEAD PUBLISHING

NAME: _____

ADDRESS: _____

CITY: _____ STATE: _____ ZIP: _____

✂ *Cut on dotted line. To order additional copies use a plain sheet of paper.*
- -

ATTENTION BUSINESSES, GROUPS, SCHOOLS AND FUND RAISER ORGANIZATIONS

This book is available at quantity discounts with

bulk purchases for businesses, fund raiser organizations,

educational or sales promotional use.

For more information write, call or fax:

Cozy Homestead Publishing

Cozy Homestead Publishing, Inc.
5425 S. Fulton-Lucas Road
Swanton, Ohio 43558
Phone: 419-826-COOK (2665)
FAX: 419-826-2700

♥♥♥♥♥♥♥♥♥♥♥♥♥♥♥♥♥♥♥♥♥♥♥♥♥♥♥♥♥

♥♥♥♥♥♥♥♥♥♥♥♥♥♥♥♥♥♥♥♥♥♥♥

If you would like to know of future recipe books written by Dawn just fill out the card below. When her next book comes out we'll be sure to let you know!

Name_____

Address _____

City _____ , State _____ , Zip _____

What I liked most about your book:
_____
_____
_____

What I'd like to see more of:
_____
_____
_____

Thanks for you encouragement!
God Bless & Good Eatin's!
Love,
Dawn

Mail To: Down Home Cookin' Without the Down Home Fat
c/o Cozy Homestead Publishers, Inc.
5425 S. Fulton-Lucas Rd.
Swanton, OH 43558

✄ —
Cut on dotted line.

If you've created your own fast and easy, extremely low fat, and delicious recipe mail it to:

Dawn Hall
c/o Cozy Homestead Publishers
5425 S. Fulton-Lucas Rd.
Swanton, Ohio 43558

Each recipe published will have a write-up and photo of its originator next to it.

♥♥♥♥♥♥♥♥♥♥♥♥♥♥♥♥♥♥♥♥♥♥♥